Diagnosis and Prescription To Combat Global Terrorism:

An Insight in
Judaism
Islam
Hinduism
Christianity and
Buddhism

Jeremiah Z. Whapoe

authorHOUSE®

AuthorHouse™
1663 Liberty Drive, Suite 200
Bloomington, IN 47403
www.authorhouse.com
Phone: 1-800-839-8640

First published by AuthorHouse 9/24/2009

ISBN: 978-1-4389-9808-4 (e)
ISBN: 978-1-4389-9806-0 (sc)
ISBN: 978-1-4389-9807-7 (hc)

Library of Congress Control Number: 2009909871

Printed in the United States of America
Bloomington, Indiana

This book is printed on acid-free paper.

TABLE OF CONTENTS

Acknowledgment

This book was written in Richton Park, Illinois exactly two years after my graduate studies at the University of Illinois at Chicago.

My three children, Jerecom M. Whapoe, Jergeor N. Whapoe, and Jerra Z. Whapoe, played individual inspirational roles in empowering me to complete this book. Jerecom stayed up late at night with me while I did research to gather valuable information that would support my arguments. During most of the nights that I stayed awake, Jerecom was with me, telling me jokes and giving me little smiles. Jergeor believed that he was my supervisor during this project; he'd go to bed early and when he'd wake up in the morning, he'd greet me in a big voice, "what's up, daddy?" The next question that followed was, "how many pages have you written?" This question usually went unanswered; I usually responded with a smile. My daughter Jerra was my advisor. She'd usually come around and ask, "Papa, how long do you have to stay up writing this book?" Then she'd say "good job" and walk away. I always waited for her sharp voice in the morning and for her two word advice – "be careful" – before she'd leave the house for school, while I take off for my eighty-minute journey to work. Jerra's advice was a constant reminder for me while I commuted back and forth to work on Interstate 294.

Heartfelt thanks to my brother, Matthew Wayker, and his wife, McVilla Wayker, who provided moral support and facilitated the production of this book, and countless thanks to Beatrice Barry and her family, who were very instrumental during my research. Ms. Barry always was in readiness to use her local library card to borrow books for me. After a long night's research, she would call in the morning and inquire about the usefulness of the books we had borrowed.

I also am grateful to my friend Karsia Donner. Ms. Donner was one of the few friends I discussed my ideas with; she served as one of my resource persons, and provided one of the first books I read on religion.

A number of friends and relatives read the manuscript in draft and provided comments and independent judgments: Julio Reyes, Wanda Teruel, Gregory Norman, my aunt, Dr. Kwekeh Doe-Subah, and Ken Keibler, who always was willing to listen to my discussion on this controversial topic. At the end of my usual three to five minutes exposé, he would ask, "What time do you have to do research after a long day's work?"

When I answered, he then would say "I think you are doing an exceptional job. I can't wait to get copy of your work." I enjoyed his candid comments and kind personality. And Arnold Friedman (aka Editor-in-Chief) of EditAvenue.com did a splendid job of copyediting the manuscript.

Finally, special thanks to the library staffs of Richton Park, Matteson, Des Plaines, and Arlington Heights, Illinois, who always were eager to recommend materials that would support my ideas being dispensed in the book. Countless thanks to you all for making this journey a success.

About the Book

Have you ever wondered about the rise of global terrorism? Have you ever thought about finding a solution to terrorism? Are you worried about the next 9/11? Have you been concerned about the threat America and its allies are experiencing from Islamic extremists? Is terrorism your concern and do you wish to gain insight into the psychology of terrorists? Do you want to know why terrorism is perpetuating in the world? In short, are you concerned about your own security and that of your loves ones and hope that the world becomes a peaceful place for humankind? If your answer to any of these questions is yes, then this book will provide the answers to your inquiries on global terror.

Diagnosis and Prescription to Combat Global Terrorism attempts to bring you the undisclosed facts or realities about terrorism that government officials, politicians, and religious leaders are yet to discuss in the public realm. The book discusses terrorism from insights gained in the world's five major religions (Judaism, Islam, Hinduism, Christianity, and Buddhism) and describes how these religions' culture, beliefs, or doctrines are crucial to enhancing democracy – or infecting the world with chaos, desperation, and uncertainty.

This book brings new ideas from four different schools of thought (Psychology, Political Science, Sociology, and Social Work) to help you digest critical information about the rise of global terror. The book also recommends ways to combat this ill societal phenomenon. The author uses an intellectual ideological microscope to magnify the unspoken underlying causes of global terrorism; he provides theoretical explanations on how religions and cultures impact terrorism as well as have the ability to deter the current divide.

While the contents of this book are exploratory and stimulating to its general readers, it also can be used in colleges and universities in academic disciplines such as Political Science, Religious Studies, Sociology, and Psychology to model the way for a violence-free democratic society.

ABOUT THE AUTHOR

The author is an emerging thinker in the Political Science, Sociology, Social Work, and Divinity disciplines with impartial pristine views on controversial and sensitive issues that tend to affect humankind.

As a young man, Jeremiah always had sophisticated views on how individual orientations, be they religious, political, or social, had greater impacts in defining the persona of individuals. Thereby, he strongly holds the belief that individuals or groups of people from the same environmental orientation (religious, political, or cultural) would have harmonious worldviews or the same mindsets. With this as the fundamental basis of the author's scholarly thoughts, he immigrated to the United States, where he perceives opportunities for higher education that would be crucial in populating his insight about humankind. Prior to coming to the U.S., he was the first human rights activist in the Republic of Liberia. The author gave birth to human rights activism in Liberia when he lighted the "Human Rights Candle" at the United Nations Peace Building Conference in Liberia during its 14-year civil conflict.

Jeremiah holds a Bachelor of Arts Degree in Political Science with emphasis in International Politics; a Bachelor of Arts Degree in Sociology; and a Master's Degree in Social Work from the University of Illinois at Chicago. The author also teaches Human Relations at the Westwood College in Metropolitan Chicago.

The author's youth in his home country, Liberia, focused on peace building that was channeled through human rights advocacy, his collective social science disciplines, and his polemic arguments on societal ills during graduate studies that indicated a proclivity for world peace in his later life.

In this book, *Diagnosis and Prescriptions to Combat Global Terrorism: An Insight in Judaism, Islam, Hinduism, Christianity, and Buddhism*, the author brings a collection of scholarly insights from his three academic backgrounds to bring current and future global terrorism to a manageable level without perpetuating the loss of human resources from both sides of the coin (democratic torchbearers on one side and the Islamic world on the other).

This book not only offers intellectual enlightenment of the current global divide; it also will be your companion for peace; food for thought for human existence, and a legacy for social harmony.

Introduction

The world has come on a long journey and its complexity has interfaced with diversity in the human race, with considerable focus on cultures, customs, traditions, religions and any form of civilization that continues to distinguish humankind from any other species. These peculiar characteristics (cultures, customs, traditions, and religions) of humankind have evolved and become more diverse, and yet take shape with one simple definition that would gain universality. For example, culture could be defined as a way of life; tradition could be defined as a practiced behavior of the people; and religion could be defined as a cohesive conscious belief and faith practiced by the people. These definitions are not absolute; they might differ from one culture to another; from one religion to another, as well as from one language to another.

In the contextual understanding of culture, custom, tradition, and religion, there appears to be some commonality or golden thread that makes these values synonymous. The commonality identified in understanding these vernaculars is the value of the people whom they encompass. These words (culture, tradition, custom, and religion) mean that humankind has the faculty to identify in a group context how to live, what behavior to practice or accept; what belief to hold, and faith to embrace.

If you agree that humankind has the self-consciousness or faculty to choose in a group context what to believe, practice, live, and trust, then you might agree that these acceptable values (culture, tradition, custom, and religion) that are likely to differ from one group to another might have a situation in which they would be critical of each other in a group context. This means that the value of belief of one group might not be accepted by another group and vice versa. One group's certain way of life cannot disavow or disparage another group's belief or conviction.

Culture, customs, tradition, and religion are believed to be the bedrock for the way of the people. In this book, the author devoted time to bring to your consciousness the different perspectives of democracy in the context of culture, tradition, and custom in the eye of religion. After reading this book, you will understand and conceive what democracy means in the context of values (culture, tradition, custom, and religion). You will understand how democracy is practiced by individual groups as they see it. The interconnectedness of religion, culture, custom, tradition, and democracy is indistinguishable. You will discover how these values (culture, tradition, custom, and religion) are accepted and practiced in a group context and in a contextual understanding of democracy.

In order to get the author's viewpoint clearly, it is suggested that you create an open mind to position yourself as an impartial observer as you merge in depth with your reading and understand each group perspective of democracy in a value context. Your center point of judgment should be based on how individual groups choose their way of life.

Understanding Democracy in a Contextual Framework

The concept of democracy is a phenomenon assumed to be accepted by a majority of the world's population. As this phenomenon spreads and captures the minds of people around the world; one key thing that is pivotal, but yet forgotten, is that the concept (democracy) evolves from culture to culture; nation to nation, and religion to religion.

It is widely believed by all nations or world demography that democracy has two indisputable principles that are accepted by all peoples regardless of beliefs or any identities: tolerance and equality. These two principles are contextually understood in the Islamic religion and defined as consultation, consensus, and independent judgment that are inscribed in the holy Qu'ran as Shura, ijmaa, and jihad, respectively (Einfield, 2005). If the ideas of tolerance and equality that are the fulcrum of democracy are identified somehow in culture and religions from nation to nation; then it is inevitable that the idea of democracy should be dispensed in the context of culture or religion or any belief system as it evolves from nation to another. For the concept of democracy to enhance its universality, it should be treated as a value or belief.

In a broader context, democracy might be defined as government in which political control is shared by all people, either directly or by representatives whom they elect. Democracy is a practice that values social, political, and legal equality. With unlimited meaning to democracy in the modern world, democracy signifies the ultimate authority in political affairs rightfully belongs to the people.

Democracy, in short, is a concept that demonstrates the actualization of the will of the people. With this concept, it is compulsory that we acknowledge the divergence of humankind as it relates to race, color, creed, identities, gender, and religion, as these values evolve from one culture to another and from one generation to the next. This wide divergence might be understood parallel to people's beliefs that have unique characteristics related to people's identities or customs. However, to realize democracy in the context of beliefs and enhance a global destiny that would evoke the spirit of national building, there should be an idea of common interest or golden thread concerning all nations. Democracy in context will acknowledge the differences in its practice from one nation to another. For example, what are considered democratic values in Pakistan might not be considered democratic values in the United States due to differences of culture and beliefs. If democracy and culture or beliefs are parallel, they both will embrace the ideology of sovereignty of the people; government based upon the consent of the governed; majority rule; minority rights; guarantees of basic human rights; free and fair elections; equality before the law; due process of law; constitutional limits on government; social, economic, and political pluralism; and values of tolerance, pragmatism, cooperation, and compromise that continue to pillar this ideology of co-hesive society building.

DEMOCRACY AS A SYSTEM

To digest the concept of democracy, one should expand his or her thought horizon and consider this ideology (democracy) as a system that has several but different coordinated parts arranged in different ways to produce a well crafted outcome for the common good of its consumers. A system is a group or arrangement of parts, facts, phenomena, etc., that re-late or interact with each other in such a way to form or enhance a whole. If democracy should be thought about in this regard, then it should be considered in the context of its pillars as it would be defined from culture to culture, nation to nation, religion or belief to another, thereby guided by a well defined cohesive bond, tradition, or golden thread that tends to define a destiny of a geographic setting.

Since cultures or beliefs differ among geographic settings, in order to enhance a cohesive bond, the people should define the pillars of democracy in the context of their culture, custom, religion, or any bond that tends to keep them together. In the absence of contextual definition and practical-ity of democracy, the enhancement of its pillars in a conventional outlook appears to be an elusion or ideological unicorn that would be talked about but does not exist. For example, consider religious democracy: Islamic democracy might differ from Buddhist democracy as well as that of Chris-tianity; hence, that of other cultures, religions, or geographic locations. Democracy as a system will produce its crafted outcome if its pillars are defined in the context of the people's beliefs as they practice them for their own common good.

This book does not try to juxtapose democracy to beliefs; its intent is to inspire its readers on how beliefs and geographic locations shape human behaviors and conceptions, thereby making it almost impossible to conventionalize inner group beliefs on the outside group. However, the idea of arriving at a negotiated balance or manageable cooperation on the international level is underscored.

CHAPTER 1
DEMOCRACY IN THE EYE OF JUDAISM

JEWISH RELIGIOUS WORLDVIEW

Discussing democracy in the thematic expression of a religion such as Judaism, it becomes important to trace the history or origin of the religion and understand its dogmatic or evolving characteristics; hence, its envisaged future.

The origin of Judaism can be traced from the Bible; therefore its culture, values, and customs, are largely derivative of the twenty-four books of the Hebrew Bible. Facts that could validate the biblical heritage of Judaism are: the continue belief that the revealed teachings of God were given to the people of Israel in antiquity; the notion of Jews that the persons in the biblical antiquity are their own lineage; the events of biblical time periods are their own prehistory; the Jews consider that the covenant between God and the ancient Israelites is the basis of their religious obligations and the assertion that the division of the antique religion of the ancient Hebrews and contemporary Judaism, as well as the earliest organization of classical Judaism, were in fact founded by Ezra, a priest whose work is recorded in biblical history; the Jews acknowledged the beliefs and commandments in the bible that continue to impact the religion; the Jews continue to accept the laws and directions of the Bible to model their behaviors and the tradition of the religion that all future of the religion, no matter how innovative, has its ultimate source in the bible (Earhart, 1993).

Another fact about Judaism that might serve as a syllogism for our argument in discussing democracy in religious context are: the Torah, the sacred book of Judaism, is universal and its believers should encourage discipleship – a concept that contributed to the spread of Jews across the world; Judaism beholds that humans were created in the image of God, therefore teaches that life is sacrosanct; Judaism has found it difficult to give a precise description of God – Judaism's descriptions of God are mutually exhausted but metaphoric because they conceive the notion that God is above all creatures, therefore making it unrealistic to personify God as a "He or She" being; Judaism believes that in order for the universe to stand, it should be built on justice, on truth, on peace, and on prudent judgment (Atkinson, 2004, and Neusner, 1986).

These facts would channel our thoughts in a path that we impartially would analyze some basic fundamentals of the religion and compare its values with democracy and deduce a conclusion on its impacts on Jews and their response to democracy. The teachings of Genesis, Exodus, Leviticus, Numbers, Deuteronomy, etc., are all anthologies of the Bible that continue to inspire the tradition of Judaism

JUDAISM'S RESPONSE TO TIME

While it is established that Judaism derived from the Bible and behooves its teaching, it did not remain the same after the destruction of Israel and Judea by King Nebuchadnezzar in 587/6 B.C.E. After two thousand years of exile, when the Jews returned to their land to restore their religion, their rituals and religious practices were shaped by the Persians, who assumed authority in the local region. The Persians tried to encourage the Jews to divorce the practice of monotheistic ideology and adapt their Zoroastrianism, the belief in the supreme power of two Gods (God of Good and God of Evil) an idea that was detested strongly by the Jews. However, more forms of Judaic beliefs such as eschatology and angelology were shaped by Persian influence (Earhart 1993).

One may argue that these facts are not pronounced in Jewish history today; however, the Jews acknowledge that the practices, values, customs, and traditions of their religion have evolved or been impacted by time. The return of the Jews from the four corners of the globe conglomerated different ideas, but one interest. The coming together of Jews with different ideas was geared toward revisiting their religious book, the Torah, and rescuing Jews who might flee from different locations as a result of oppression around the world. After the rejuvenation of the Torah, it was considered a religious document in accordance with new historical ideas that merged with contemporary civilization. Modern Judaism came to exist as a system of thoughts and practices that mirror the historical relative time period or era and not as an inflexible document written in stone that does not acknowledge the importance of time in humans' activities.

As Earhart discussed it, the refurbishing of the Torah was intended to modify the Jewish tradition; if Judaism was no timeless essence but a perpetual historical artifact of Jewish creation, the fate of the religion was something humans could and should take responsibility for. The rejuvenation of the Jewish culture after thousands of years of exile created a coalition of interests among individuals who researched Jewish sources scientifically and those who conceived Judaism as an evolving religious cultural civilization (Earhart, 1993, and Tessler, 1994). The transformation period following the exile years of Jews was cultivated in defining mutual transition from antique Judaism to modern civilization, where the Torah will take on a new moderate religious dimension for the betterment of societal cohesiveness. The reformation established a movement known as Zionism. The basic ideology of the movement was to ensure the physical well-being and enfranchisement of Jews, when they could not rely on their host countries; and further, to rescue Jews who survived the Nazi Holocaust and Oriental Jews from Arab persecution after the national state of Israel was founded in 1948.

Judaism accepts its escape from the period in history in which its daily living was tearfully characterized, and events such as the murders of six million Jews during the Holocaust; influences of different cultures due to their being exiled in several regions such as Spain and Morocco in the West, Iraq and Iran in the East, as well as Italy and Germany. The Jews maintained their core future of traditional life that reflect the study of Torah and its interpretation, legal procedures through the fulfillment of the commandments, recognition of their responsibility to God as well as God's responsiveness to their actions, needs, and acknowledging that Israel is the chosen nation among other nations for the unification of people in just and righteous order; the repeating of the religion's core future liturgy and the belief of its people and continued reactivation of the Halakhic and Aggadic laws that interpret their fundamental values, Torah remained unchanged (Earhart, 1993). Despite the oppression the Jews endured with their enclaves in different regions, they continue to promote the principles of social tolerance and kindness. The preservation of these Jewish principles remained a critical factor in explaining why their religious practices, values, customs, and mores easily reconcile with basic democratic pillars and continue to impact their behavior. Jews founded their religion on traditional teaching and belief in the 613 commandment that are referred to as the Mitzvoth and are elaborated in the Torah or the Old Testament. The mitzvoth teach about social justice, a tradition that commits the Jews to engage in charitable endeavors with respect to enhancing life and people's well-being. The Jews believe that they hold the responsibility to behold God's requirement that emphasizes justice, love, and kindness. Social justice, which is an integral part of human rights that also is embedded in democracy, is a nucleus of Jewish orientations. Ancient historical accounts, such as Prophet Amos's denunciation of the mistreatment of the poor; the Jewish teaching that obligates all Jews to practice justice and mercy; and the repetitious Jewish teaching of love and forgiveness throughout their history, are evidence that could bring the religion closer to democracy.

Jewish behaviors are the direct product of their environment, orientation, and beliefs (culture, tradition, customs, or religion). The Jews' reactions to democracy are based exactingly on their beliefs. The central idea that shapes the Jews' thoughts and perception of democracy is their orientation based on their religion. The true Jews indoctrinate their children with their religious beliefs that elaborate peace and tolerance. Judaism has been parallel with democracy because of its indoctrinating philosophy that teaches young people the fundamentals of the religion that relate to morals and interconnectedness of people. Judaism is not a religion that focuses its teaching on its believers going to heaven after life and thereby taking responsibility to guide them through the process. Judaism is an earthly-centered religion that teaches ideas and values that would make the earth a better place where wholesome society would be achieved. It believes in afterlife; however, its teaching does not focus on preparing humankind for the next world. Judaism focuses its teaching on ethics and ideals that encourages every believer to seek God's approval in everything he/she does.

It can be suggested that the doctrine of the Jewish religion that focuses on making Earth a better place for all is another reason why the religion is parallel to democracy in its practices. Hence, Judaism has several characteristics that help to unite its religious philosophy with democracy. The Jewish religion believes that the Jews are the chosen people of God, an idea that is not viewed as a privilege but a responsibility to be servants to God to bring all his people of the world to him, detest idolatry, man-made images, and false ideas. The religion also believes that humankind was made in the image of God with liberty to choose between good and evil at any point in time of life. The concept that man was made in God's image, and acknowledgement that God is a loving God, helps those who practice this religion to learn the love for their fellow human beings. One could argue that the teaching of Judaism that is based on the Torah – the first five books of the Old Testament inspired by the Prophet Moses – teaches vengeance or retribution as the story of Moses details in the holy Bible. However, the word Torah also stands for all the Hebrew Scriptures and all the laws based on it. Moreover, the Torah strongly believes in the teaching of the Prophet Moses in Exodus that revealed the Ten Commandments:

> *I am the Lord thy God who brought you out of Egypt to be your god; thou shalt not have other gods before me. Thou shalt not make unto thee any graven image, or any likeness of any thing that is in heaven above, or that is in the earth beneath, or that is in the water under the earth: thou shalt not bow down thyself to them, nor serve them: for I the Lord thy God am a jealous God, visiting the iniquity of the fathers upon the children unto the third and fourth generation of them that hate me; and showing mercy unto thousands of them that love me, and keep my commandments. Thou shalt not take the name of the Lord thy God in vain. Remember the Sabbath day, to keep it holy. Six days shalt thou labor, and do all thy work: But the seventh day is the Sabbath of the Lord thy God: in it thou shalt not do any work, thou, nor thy son, nor thy daughter, thy manservant, nor thy maidservant, nor thy cattle, nor thy stranger that is within thy gates: for in six days the Lord made Heaven and Earth, the sea and all that in them is, and rested the seven day: wherefore the Lord blessed the Sabbath day, and hallowed it. Honour thy father and thy mother: that thy days may be long upon the land which the Lord thy God giveth thee. Thou shalt not kill. Thou shalt not commit adultery. Thou shalt not steal. Thou shalt not bear false witness against thy neighbors. Thou shalt not covet thy neighbor's house, thou shalt not covet thy neighbor's wife, nor his manservant, nor his maidservant, nor his ox, nor his ass, nor any thing that is thy neighbor's And all the people saw the thundering, and the lightnings, and the noise of the trumpet, and the mountain smoking: and when the people saw it, they removed, and stood afar off. And they said unto Moses, speak thou with us and we will hear: but*

*let not God speak with us, lest we die. And Moses said unto
the people, fear not: for God is come to prove you and that
his fear may be before your faces, that ye sin not (The Holy
Bible: Exodus 20).*

While one may argue that the Prophet Moses taught vengeance and
retribution, such as "an eye for an eye," the Ten Commandments of Moses
that inspires the doctrine of Judaism also teach tolerance and rule of law that
are pivotal to democracy. The commandments also taught neighborliness.
Another doctrine of the Jewish religion that is based on the teaching of the
Prophet Isaiah that pronounced peace amongst people and all nations:

*And it shall come to pass in the last days, that the mountain
of the Lord's house shall be established in the tip of the mountains, and shall be exalted above the hills; and all nations shall
flow unto it. And many people shall go and say, come ye, and
let us go up to the mountain of the Lord, to the house of the
God of Jacob; and he will teach us of his ways, and we will
walk in his path: for out of Zion shall go forth the law and the
word of the Lord from Jerusalem. And he shall judge among
the nations, and shall rebuke many people: and they shall beat
their swords into plowshares, and their spears into pruning
hooks: nations shall not lift up sword against nations; neither
shall they learn war any more (The Holy Bible: Isaiah 2).*

This teaching of the Prophet Isaiah that also is indoctrinated into
Judaism pronounced peace and tolerance; hence, a philosophy that continues to impact the believers of Judaism. Judaism is not discussed here as
the only religious icon for democracy; however, the religion is being discussed in the context in which its doctrines and beliefs continue to impact
democracy. The discussion tries to enlighten individuals how religion has
an inescapable impact on the dispensation of democratic values around
the world and shaping human's behavior.

JEWISH TRADITION AS A CONDUIT TO DEMOCRACY

In the Jewish tradition, five belief principles are practiced to orient
the boy child with details and values of the Jewish culture when the boy
reaches age thirteen. The T'filin, Aliyah, Torah, Parent's Blessing Seudah,

and the Derasha are core principles that serve as behavioral determinants for true Jews (Wood 1987). These five principles, without detailing them individually, all focus on introducing the boy child to the real values and behaviors of a Jews.

Besides these five orientation principles, thirteen other conducts or principles of faith that were formulated by Rabbi Moses ben Maimon in the twelfth century continue to direct the Jewish tradition:

1. *God has, does, and will create everything*
2. *God is one*
3. *God is not and does not have a body*
4. *God is the first and the last*
5. *It is wrong to pray to anyone or anything apart from God*
6. *The works of the prophets are true*
7. *The prophecy of Moses is true and he is the greatest of the prophets*
8. *The Torah was given to Moses*
9. *The Torah will never be changed*
10. *God knows everything – everyone's thoughts and acts*
11. *God rewards those who keep his commandments and punishes those who break them*
12. *The Messiah will come*
13. *There will be a resurrection of the dead (Atkinson 2004 and Wood 1987).*

Due to the polyvalent linguistic, political, cultural transient of experiences that permeated Jewish traditions over the years, their religious laws evolved from Mosaic law to contemporary civilization, where political tolerance, pluralism, rule of law, and freedom of expression are championing their society. The development of the Jewish tradition and the mutuality of its religious values with democracy do not ignore the several eruptions of violence between Israel and its surrounding Arab neighboring states. The discussion acknowledged the Six-Day War that began on June 6, 1967, in which Israel defeated Egypt, Syria, and Jordan and occupied the Sinai Peninsula and the Egyptian-controlled Gaza Strip, plus the Golan Heights and East Jerusalem; Israel's invasion of Lebanon in June of 1982 with the intent to restore peace in Galilee, etc. (Tessler 1994). The Jewish religious record discussed here tries to pronounce the big picture of the

Jewish religion being flexible to modify over the years some of its religious practices and hold on to teachings of societal peace such as Halakhah that elaborates humanitarianism.

> *The Halakhah teaches the highest esteem for manual work, and contains progressive regulations for the protection of labor which are unrivaled even by the most modern legislation. It is merciful in its penal code, tending toward the abolition of capital punishment, conceiving of legal penalties not as vengeance but as protection for society and treating crime more as a pathological phenomenon than anything else....Restricting private ownership in the interest of public welfare, it calls for a most liberal social order. It considers ethical family life as a prerequisite for a happy society (Federbush in Tessler 1994).*

The teaching of the Jewish religious Halakhah that characterizes liberalism or welfare of the people and loathes violence is one reason why the Jews find solace in the pillars of democracy.

Democracy in the eye of Judaism is based principally on Jews' beliefs and faith in their God. Hence, their behaviors in the outside world could be the reflection of how they see, believe, and worship; and the faith or devotion they have in their God. One important pillar of democracy that seems to stem from the tradition of Judaism is pluralism. However, there appears to be minimum cohesion between Judaism and democratic pluralism. Judaism is somehow pluralistic in respect to acknowledging that there exist separate identities (beliefs, cultures, or customs) of different nations. This idea of recognizing diversity is avowed in the Jewish political tradition as Jews see that the people of the world or other nations to have the right to life and self-governance under their faith or God. This consciousness of Jews draws a clear distinction between Judaism on one hand and Christianity and Islam on the other. Judaism is a tolerant religion that does not embark on enhancing the hegemony of a single world state or homogeneity in principle as well as unity in which all nations' religions or faiths are obliterated or transformed to one single universal belief. Judaism believes that the world should be a place where all nations recognize the sovereignty of God; however, they should maintain or hold the right to separate national characteristics with respect to religion, culture, customs, traditions, or beliefs.

On the other side of the spectrum, Judaism has a skewed belief about individuals or nations that might distinguish them from being part of any religion (Islam, Christianity, Buddhism, Hindu, and Judaism, etc.). Democratic pluralism that recognizes all forms or ways is somehow blurry in the eye of Judaism with respect to paganism. While Judaism acknowledges pluralism in values, religion, culture, and beliefs among nations and people, it does not recognize paganism (Wood 1987). Judaism acknowledges the democratic value of freedom of choice whereby individuals or nations as entities would choose to worship God in any form or manner without judgment; however, it also holds that God has the responsibility to determine which form of worship is pleasant or acceptable in his (God's) sight.

Notwithstanding, the Jews strongly denounce the ideology proclaimed by both Christianity and Islam that as a believer in God, you automatically are on the battlefront for God to gain supremacy over unbelievers (Kressel 2002). It is not disputable that there are individuals whose behaviors are not acceptable in religious faith; however, the Jewish religion does not believe that it is the responsibility of humankind to fight for God's dominion over those who refuse to proclaim his might.

Self-governance is one of the strongest pillars of the Jewish religion. Jewish political culture derived from the Bible, where it is believed that autonomy is determined by God; hence, the governance of mankind is in the hands of the people within the structure divinity of God. In the Old Testament, God confirmed his relationship with the people through a covenant in which he played a pivotal role in structuring the religious and moral behaviors of the people. However, the holy scripture of the Jews (Torah) specifies that there is no one chosen regime that is perfect; it is up to the people to establish an appropriate political system that will meet the moral, social, and religious requirements that would govern them. The Torah believes that it is suitable for a political system to be established, be just, have a focus that is evenhandedness and provide care for the needy, and hold the religious doctrine of the Jewish nation, hence interpreted by the judicial system of the time. One of the important values of the Torah is that it acknowledges that leadership should be republican-oriented whereby laws that would govern the people should be popularly consented by those in governance.

There is no uncertainty about the democratic values of the Jewish polity that spelled out free choice of the people; however, on the other hand, Judaism has certain aristocratic traces due to the prominent role it gives to leadership in the higher strata with regard to priests, prophets, and others that had responsibilities for interpreting the Torah; nevertheless, acknowledging shared power among higher strata of the religion. While Judaism is dignified by it democratic principles, its distribution of power that channels through the noblest gives rise to oligarchic dominance in Jewish leadership in Israel and other Jewish communities around the world. Despite this skewed character of the Jewish religion, it popularly holds the belief that government should be constituted and changed by the people without distinction to gender, age, or any form of identity that would limit the people's involvement in making decision regarding the function of their government.

The perfection of the Jewish religion's embracement of democratic principles sometimes becomes questionable when autocracy's supremacy becomes pronounced in religious culture, for example, the biblical story of King Herod's autocratic dominance of ancient Jews, notwithstanding that the Jews may argued that the regime of Herod was imposed by the Romans.

DEMOCRATIC ORIENTATION AND JUDAISM

The democratic tradition of the Jewish religion is crystallized in three dimensions in their holy scripture know as crown and in Hebrew as Ketarim. In Torah, the Ketarim is responsible for communicating God's command to the people and interpreting the Torah as constitution to the people; Kehunah, commonly known as the priesthood, is responsible for being a medium from the people to God; and Malkhut, which is known as civil rule, is responsible for the everyday activities of civil governance. These three major dimensions of Jewish leadership values might be interpreted as parallel to the three branches of government (executive, legislative, and judiciary) that is popularly instituted by nations that profess democracy around the world. In spite of some history of power difficulties among the three Jewish branches of power (Ketarim, Kehunah, and Malkhut) in dispensation of power or responsibilities, the branches of government always have participated actively in the governance of Jewish political history in the local arena to the people as a whole. Hence, in the agreement linking Judaism and democracy, on a popular note, the competition has to be viewed in the light of separation of power and division of responsibilities, and consent and inclusion of the people governed, not distinctly on skewed religious tradition. Vitally, the rules of politics, the responsibilities of the leadership to the people, and a suitable allotment of power among the leadership are characteristics of Judaism that could be considered the foundation on which democracy was formulated. If democracy and Judaic values are duplicates of the other, then it will be difficult to draw distinctions between the two except for their nomenclatures and geographic origins; Judaism derives from the East, democracy from the West.

If democracy should be considered as a conduit through which unity will emerge among nations, including those in the East, it should include the values of all religions. Its philosophy should be in the middle and not skewed to the left or right. The notion in the East that is popular with Islamism is that democracy is skewed to the right; this means that it endorses the values of Judaism and Christianity, which have common values; hence, a crucial point that appears to ostracize the inclusion of other Islamic religious values, thereby making it difficult for democracy to gain universal popularity. Considering the context and gradual procedures that complemented the integration of Judaism into modern civilization's values – democracy – it was through incremental changes that occurred from within the religion realm. The changes occurred with no or less obliteration of life or property due to the linguistic, cultural, and traditional diversity of the inner group. While the inner group was interested in preserving the Jewish tradition/religion, at the same time, it was interested in finding a negotiated balance that would bring scattered Jews who have been corrupted by other cultures or religions from across the globe to keep them together. In a rational consideration, one might see the Jews as a nation and Israel as a melting pot where all Jews who fled would return for rescue and to help resurrect their values. Another important factor that impacted the Jewish transformation period was considering the content of the Torah in accordance with the time period; thereby, the essence of time gave room for religious scholars to rethink the book and merge its contents with today's civilization.

Next, we focus on the camera in which Islam sees democracy and cardinal points or issues that might be its focal points of deviance.

CHAPTER 2
DEMOCRACY IN THE EYE OF ISLAM

THE CORE BELIEFS OF ISLAM

In our contemporary society, especially in the West, it might seem an anachronism to some people when one tries to discuss democracy in the same paragraph with Islam. This doubt is becoming literal stemming from several terrorist incidents around the world that are said to be orchestrated by Islamic extremists. However, to understand democracy from the Islamic point of view, we must be able to explore the five fundamental principles or pillars of the religion.

Shahada is the first pillar or principle of Islam. The word Shahada is an Arabic word meaning bearing testimony. This pillar holds all Islam believers or Muslims to profess and confirm in public the oneness or supremacy of God. This principle of testifying also teaches the Muslim a sense of legal morality when it comes to crediting or borrowing money from each other. The Qu`ran teaches that in every monetary transaction between Muslims there should be at least two witnesses who will acknowledge the transaction; hence to serve as witness in case there arises any form of dispute.

The second pillar is the Salat. The Salat has many explanations in Arabic; however, for the context of our study, we will refer to one of its meaning that considers it an act of prayer by Muslims. This pillar is regarded as the nuclear or foundation for which Islam stands. To the Muslims, the Salat is more important in God's sight than any other act being practiced in the religion as indicated by the Qu`ran:

> O you who believe, remember Allah with much remembrance, and glorify him morning and evening. He it is who sends blessings on you and (so do) his angels, that he may bring you forth out of darkness into light. And he is ever merciful to the believers. Their salutation on the day they meet him will be, peace! And he has prepared for them an honorable reward. O Prophet, surely we have sent thee as a witness, and a bearer of good news and a Warner and as

an inviter to Allah by his permission, and as a light-giving
sun. And give the believers the good news that they will have
great grace from Allah (33:41-47).

Evidently, the Muslims are known to practice this pillar or principle frequently, even in public places. Islam believes that praying without season or performing the Shahada will bring them closer to God, bless them, and their sins will be forgiven. The Salat has four different spheres or strata that will not be discussed here. However, all the stages of the Salat have the purpose of purification or improving the relationship between humankind and God. The third pillar is the Zakat. As tithe is in the Bible, the Zakat is an act of giving certain percentage of income for charitable purposes. According to the Qu'ran there are eight different categories of people that should benefit from the Zakat:

(Zakat) Charity is only for the poor and the needy, and those
employed to administer it, and those whose hearts are made
to incline (to truth), and (to free) the captives, and those in
debt, and in the way of Allah and for the wayfarer-an ordi-
nance from Allah. And Allah is knowing, wise (9:60).

An important point to emphasize about Zakat is that, unlike the previous two pillars we have discussed, Zakat is not mandatory upon Muslims to perform. In order to be obligated to perform the Zakat or make charitable donation, an individual has to acquire profit from his or her business or any means of income. Without these conditions, Muslims can choose not to perform Zakat. Zakat is encouraged in Islam to promote social interaction and at the same time to purify one's possessions in the presence of God. In other words, performing Zakat is a choice of an individual to purify his or her own belongings in the sight of God and ask God for blessing and protection for his or her material possession.

Fasting is the fourth pillar. This pillar usually is performed during the month of Ramadan. Ramadan is the ninth month of the Islamic calendar during which believers collectively fast and pray together. The fifth and the last pillar is the Hajj. The fifth pillar is performed during the last lunar month of the year when all Muslims from all walks of life make pilgrimage to the holy land (Mecca). The last pillar also is not obligatory upon the believers; however, every Muslim is urged to attend the ceremony at least once in his or her life before death. The Hajj is performed only in Mecca once every year.

Evidently, besides these five fundamental principles of Islam; Muslim scholars have ascribed Jihad to become the sixth pillar of Islam. As we will discuss later, Jihad by definition evolves from the third pillar (Zakat) or charity giving. We will explore later how these pillars' interpretations, especially the Zakat, have manifested and shaped Muslims' response to democracy

THE REALITY OF ISLAM VS THE REALITY OF DEMOCRACY

Several questions come to mind when democracy is being discussed in the Islamic religion. The voice of democracy is so loud that it is almost impossible to comprehend why some groups or individuals refuse to hear it. Is it possible for people to investigate the precision of the speed when it relates to those for whom it is intended, or is the sound so loud that it irritates the consciousness of the target groups? What is wrong with democracy and why is it almost becoming a failure in the Middle East? Is it the message, the messenger, or the manner in which the message is being delivered? These are questions that might come to the minds of critical thinkers who are interested in the enhancement of global peace. At the end of this chapter, you will have come up with the answer or solution that will give us insight on the limitations that democracy has had and has yet to be acknowledged.

The New Webster's Concise Dictionary defines religion as a belief in a divine or superhuman power or principles usually thought of as the creator of all things; this belief is manifested in worships, practices, and holding those values that connect the believers to the religion. Islam is one of the world's fastest spreading and popular religions whose members appear to hold strongly the several values of their beliefs. Let's bring forth some fundamental beliefs of the Islamic religion that might allude to their being cynical to the ideology of democracy. Islam conceived the belief that democracy derives from the West and has principles dominated by the values of Christianity; the pillars of democracy are infested with Jewish values; it is American ideology; its preachers are partial in a sense that they do not admit the illegal occupation of the Arabian Peninsula, the holy land of the Islamic religion (Phares, 2007 and Kressel, 2002). The ideological conception that democracy is skewed in the direction of certain religions and thus exemplified in its perceived unjust practice to the Muslim world might be the foundation for which Islam is yet to participate in the joy of freedom or democracy. Islamic values and democracy appears identical but moving in opposing directions. Islam agrees with democracy. On another front, Islam has not boarded the democratic boat because of the ideology of creating a universal homogeneous religion in which people of the world will believe and worship one God as defined by the Islamic religion (Ali M., 1994).

The correlation between Islam and democracy or free will of the people in the modern world is yet to be identified; however, one value that is quiet but loud in its practice among the preachers of democracy, Islam, and Christianity is institutional validity of their individual beliefs or in sociological terms, ethnocentrism or egotistic ideology that exists internally. For example, the Islamic religion believes that the notion of popular sovereignty contradicts the fundamental Islamic assertion of the omnipotence of the most high; hence, seeing as a form of veneration for another superior. However, there still is a debate among Muslims that their fundamental principles and values have strong correlation with those of democracy. The debate of democratic principles being compatible with religious values is not peculiar to Islam. All religions have undeniable beliefs that represent major bodies of ideas, visions, and conceptions fundamental to understanding and validating humankind and destiny. One principle or belief that is popular among religions is reincarnation of the body or resurrection of the dead during end time/so called judgment day. The faith that holds this belief also holds that God will judge and recompense individuals according to their commitment to their religious beliefs and how well they practice them (Ali M., 1994). Many of these important concepts have been used in different ways in different periods of history. The Christian traditions in pre-modern times hold the conceptual base for the divine right of monarchy; hence, in contemporary times, this belief has evolved and it is nurturing the idea that Christianity and democracy are compatible. Without any form of doubt within religious groups, each group will argue strongly that there are fundamental principles or ideological creeds in every religion that are compatible with democracy. Also, others share values that encouraged absolute monarchy or dominance of some group due to opportunity or some form of strata.

Islam believes that its values or customs are directly representative of democracy; however, it might not be spelled out word to word as in Western democracy. Muslims believe that they practice democracy in the context of the religion and the way of life of the people who believe in the religion. The amalgamation of spirituality and government builds on a fundamental affirmation at the heart of Islam. For example, the assertion that there is no divinity but God and the affirmation of God's irreversibility is the nucleus of the religion. With this tradition that the religion is build on God's divinity and omnipotence, the Islamic religion differs from the democratic concept of separating God from government. Islam holds that the ideology of separating religion from politics creates a spiritual vacuum in the public arena and opens the way for political systems that have no sense of moral values, thereby giving rise to secular states that allow the abuse of power and to Muslim societies such as the regime of Saddam Hussein in Iraq. These two examples and many more around the world may justify the suspicions Islam has of Western democracy and separating religion from politics. With respect to the Islamic doctrine, if democratic principles can be contextualized and dispensed around the globe in the context of people's culture, it will capture the attention and mind of the world, thereby creating a negotiated balance where people will live in their individual places in peace. The concept of God's divinity or oneness is called Tawhid, a holy doctrine of the Islamic religion that provides the foundation for the idea that one cannot separate different aspects of life into different compartments (Phares, 2007).

ISLAM'S DEMOCRATIC HARMONY WITH THE QUR'AN

The Islam-based democracy advocates' argument with Western democracy advocates that the Muslim world governance is parallel with democracy is evident in their Qur'an. The Qur'an considers the uprights as individuals who dispense leadership in close consultation with Shura (42:38 Qur'an). The consultative ideology of leaders among Muslims was inherited from Prophet Muhammad, who made it obligatory that all sayings and actions of the believers of Islam in managing their political affairs should be in mutual consultation with the Qur'an. This concept that perpetuates the oneness of God in every aspect of humankind makes it almost difficult for contemporary conservatives Muslim to find common ground with Western democracy, which promotes independence of government/politics from religion. If the assertion of Muslims that to have a functioning democratic system is to divorce the ideology of separating politics from religion, it will be necessary to examine some successful governments of the Muslim world that are governed by consultation with religion.

If democracy is to impact the world, especially the Middle East, it should understand the difficulties of transitioning from one way of life to another. After years of adaptation or heredities of ideology and customs, it is sometimes impossible to embrace new idea or philosophy that would one way or the other extinguish the inherited culture. The concept of experiencing difficulties with transitioning is commonplace with religion/faith or beliefs. When Islam was introduced by Muhammad in 610 AD in his hometown of Quraysh in Mecca, the idea of new religion that pronounced the belief in one God or monotheistic was strongly detested for several reasons. The people of Muhammad's town detested the idea of new religion because they believe in idols worship; and were not willing to give up their values; they also rejected the introduction of Islam because the acceptance of the new religion would denied them from financial benefits that were acquired annually during pilgrimages that brought people from all over the Arabia region; hence, an introduction of new religion that would shadow their inherited philosophy and mindset of their values was an abomination (Schwartz, S., 2002).

Muhammad was indirectly imposed into exile with violence against him and his followers by antagonists to new ideology of worship in a nearby tribal region of Yathrib, where he remained and preached the gospel on monotheistic affirmation of one God. After Muhammad immigrated to Yathrib, which today is popularly known as Medina, his ideas become popular among the townspeople and he was invited to govern the town; his ascendance to leadership was an affirmation that in order to have a successful leadership, it should be in consultation with the holy scripture or religion, an idea that is not popular in Western democracy. Muhammad's assumption of power in Yathrib was a result of civil unrest among the Yathribites that prompted their yearning for a righteous figure that could reduce the feuds among them (Schwartz, 2002). Muhammad's leadership in Yathrib or today's Medina was complemented by preaching of monotheistic ideas that inspired the people more and more and benefited from Muhammad's doctrine of peace among the people regardless of their religion.

The transformation of idolatry worship to that of monotheistic philosophy was not imposition of ideas of an individual will; but it was an idea that was gradually accepted by the people as they discovered the significance of the message and the trustworthiness of the messenger. While it was true that Muhammad was dismayed and disdained with idolatry worship that gained prominence among his people, he at the same time engaged the world and embraced life or people's way of living as it existed. The transformation of idolatry worship to monotheistic or Muhammadanism was a process that embarked on a smooth transition but not an event that demanded automatic change. The democratic idea that endorses the separation of religion from politics is viewed by true Muslims as abandonment of the agreement Muhammad made when Yathrib was changed to Medina. The agreement is consider as the first written document of good governance of Islam, which defined the principle of worship as an obligation, arbitration, and mediation. These principles have evolved and become the fulcrum of modern Islam civilization. Governing, even fighting wars with consultation of the Holy Scripture, is a belief Muslims find difficult to ignore. The Muslim ideology of governing by the inspiration of the scripture was evident during the war between idolaters of Quraysh and the converted Quraysh, who became the followers of Muhammad and flee to Yathrib. Muhammad religious leadership was tested by a series of wars between Quraysh of Mecca and Muslims of Medina; the Quraysh outnumbered the Muslims of Medina during the war but the Muhammad troops that were less in number won the war, thereby affirming the Islamic philosophy of governing with the consultation of the Holy Scripture (Ali M., 1994, & Schwartz, 2002).

RELIGIOUS TRADITION AND HUMAN RESPONSE TO DEMOCRACY

The preservation and respect of culture, beliefs, religion, customs, traditions, or values are significant in describing the persona of individual, community or group of people. The tradition of Islamic worship that emphasizes obligation, arbitration, and mediation is considered as a contract between God and the believers of Islam; thus, it continues to impact how decisions are made among the believers. On the other hand,

Muslim extremists have defined the Islamic pillar (obligation) to suit their own worldview regarding monotheistic ideology. The Jihad movement in Islam has since had a hold on the Islamic creed of obligation to serve as the military arm of the religion. The Jihad is said to be the evolved military of Muhammad that fought the idolaters or non- Islamic believers who were hostile to Muhammad during the birth of the religion in the Arabia region (Fregosi, 1998). Taking you back in time, in 622 AD, the conflict between the people of Mecca and the Yathribes was squarely on the ideology of the people holding to their accustomed values. The introduction of a philosophy that denounced multiple superpowers/idols and pronounced monotheistic ideology was perceived to deny the Yathribes of their idolatrous practices that permits them to have personal gains. As the birth of Islam was a new idea that came under strong criticism and rejection by Prophet Muhammad's own townspeople, and further evoked dispute between Mecca/Quraysh and Yathrib/Medina is as the germination or dispensation of democracy from the west to the rest of the world; democracy, than in the sight of Muslim extremist or the military arm of Islam is an idea that would be consequential of depriving Muslims several rights and benefits such as financial wealth, multiple wives or politics of governance with the consultation of religion they have fought and acquired several centuries ago (Fregosi, 1998 & Schwartz, 2002).

Few life phenomena are identified to make individuals part of a community; preservation of culture and religion, if there are not more. In some cultures, individuals are ostracized from their community if they are observed to have opposing views on established values or ideas that are fundamental to the group they belong. The concept of ostracizing individuals due to their extreme beliefs or practices is also common in the religious realm; especially, religion that does not encourage tolerance. The idea of excluding people from their niche and fighting for God has created a situation in Islam where individuals are less likely to follow their own faculty; but hold onto ideals of a group, even if they have dissimilar views of the culture or religious values and practices.

CONCERTED IDEOLOGY OF EXTREMISM

Today's world conflict stemmed from two grandiose ideologies: aggrandizement in an effort to gain superiority over people and their ideas, and movement to validate the superiority of ones beliefs, culture, government, or religion (Nye Jr., 2002). These two concepts are the nucleus of transnational conflicts. These concepts are also protected by barricade of religious beliefs. Judaism, Hinduism, Christianity, Islam, Buddhism, and other world religions have individual paths in which they validate their interest. The paths are regulated by laws of individual deity. With the different path in which religion profess to validated its interest means that people will by their religious orientations protect their spiritual, emotional and physical territories. The manner or pattern in which a religion chooses to protect these ideologies is exclusively dependent on the doctrine of the religion. Every religion has its own path in which it protects its doctrine. In Islam Jihad is the religious arm that is in the forefront of protecting the legacy of Islam. However, the protection of Islam's legacy has been manipulated with extreme ideologies that in itself appeared to do more harm than good to the religion. The harm being afflicted on Islam and other religions by and large by extremists is perpetuating because the extreme idea is being dispensed in blasphemous context in that the idea of military jihad is in the interest of Islam deity.; hence, those who believe in the Islamic deity are more likely to give some of support (emotional, spiritual, financial or physical) to the Jihadic idea since the idea is perceived to accomplish Allah's command.

There are nine thoughts that have clenched individuals to violent Jihad campaign around the world: the notion in Islam that non-Muslims who are referred to in Islam as non-believers will dominate the world if military Jihad is not enforced; the enforcement of military Jihad assures or vindicates celestial power in Islam; the practice of military Jihad will prevent Islam believers from going to hell; the practice of military Jihad is a fulfillment of God's duty and responding to his command; practicing military Jihad is an effort to validate and behold the culture of the religion from its first day of inception around 600 B.C. E. and at the same time passing on the legacy of the first prophet, Mohammad; practicing military Jihad is accomplishing divine mandate of establishing Islam empire as it happened in so many parts of the world in places such as the Arabian Peninsula and Northern Africa; to protect those that are converted to Islam; accomplish martyr for the sake of God, and abiding conventional democratic values is to the Islam as being converted to Christianity as well as avoiding Jihad in Islam faith is analogous to apostasy which is punishable by death in the Islam faith (Nye Jr., 2002 and Gunaratna, 2002).

Whatever, the reason for supporting military Jihad, what remains crucial and continues to be the seed of controversy among democracy torchbearers on one hand and the Islamic world on the other hand is the Sharia law that is said to be core value of true Muslim; hence, a pivot which makes it religiously legal and obligatory. The punishments that are associated with Sharia law have made and will continue to make it difficult for democratic values and Islamic doctrines to take common journey. The idea behind Islam extremism is to preserve the religion and conventionalize Sharia, Islam divine laws (Nasr, 2002). As Nasr indicated in his book, "to act islamically is to act in defense" and such defense has diverse path that includes but not limited to violence (Nasr, 2002:107). Violation of any provision of the Sharia law by Muslims or non-Muslims who live within Islamic states are subject to punitive measures such as imprisonment or amputation of hands or feet in the case of theft, thus depending on the value and number of item stolen. However, before any of these punishments is afflicted on an individual, two male witness or a male witness and two female would have to validate the theft allegation and the act must meet the requirements: there must have been criminal intent to take private property; item(s) stolen must be taken from a concealed or well protected place; the item(s) stolen must meet a criteria value that is determined by Islamic law and such item must not belong to family member of the theft; the theft must not be the consequent of hunger; and the theft must have criminal intent (Qur'an 5:38).

There also are punishments inflicted on adulterers and fornicators. Individuals who fornicate or commit adultery are subjected to Idreb, which means beating which the Sharia limit it to one hundred leashes for the offender (Qur'an 24:13). These laws and many other laws that are practice are validated by the religion's scripture. Sharia laws are widely known to contradict human rights and democratic values. However, before these punishments are enforced, there must be four male witnesses who will testify that they saw the accused in the act or the accused must confess her guilt. Ironically, the Sharia adultery and fornication punishment is almost usually afflicted on women. Out of curiosity one might ask, are women the only adulteress in Islam? What is the specific reason that the witness in violation of Sharia law has to be male gender focused? Feminists could argue that this provision of the Sharia law was unjustly humanly intended to subdue women to men's authority. Sharia law is considered cruel and inhuman by countries who promote democratic values. In spite of the outcry and condemnations around the world from human rights groups and countries that value democracy, it has been difficult for this law to be refined or modified because it is backed by the holy Qur`an and Islam continues to be resolute to this belief.

It was discussed earlier in our previous chapter that human behavior is a product of their culture, religion, their orientation principles or other factors in their immediate environment. Since individuals are defined by their culture or faith, Islam extremists continuously use the scripture as an instrument to mobilize Islam believers in the confine of their faith to accomplish their extreme ideologies. These ideologies are dispensed through Islamic proclamations or fatwa that are being populated by Osama bin Laden in Al Qaeda. For example, Osama continue to issue Fatawas to blaspheme Muslims and put them under the pretense that he and his followers' terrorist mission is in accordance with Allah's command.

The sentiment of excluding nonbelievers from among so-called believers is popular among the Muslims; thereby, being used as a powerful tool to involve Islam believers to engage in ideals or ideologies that are considered counterproductive. The fear to be banished from a group or custom by individuals in the Islamic religion is been used by Muslim extremists to introduce religious creed or Fatwa such as the ones being issued by bin Laden that obligates every Muslims to kill Americans and other Westerns who are allies to America and thus support democratic values and principles. In Bin Laden's fatwa that has gained prominence among Jihad frontrunners, he states that:

> *For more than seven years the United States is occupying the lands of Islam in the holiest of its territories, Arabia, Plundering its riches, overwhelming its rulers, humiliating its people, threatening its neighbors, and using its bases in the peninsula as a spearhead to fight against the neighboring Islamic peoples.*

> *Though some in the past have disputed the true nature of this occupation, the people of Arabia in their entirety have now recognized it.*

23

There is not better proof of this than the continuing American aggression against the Iraqi people, launched from Arabia despite its rulers, who all oppose the use of their territories for this purpose but are subjugated.

Despite the Immense destruction inflicted on the Iraqi people at the hands of the Crusader Jewish alliance, and in spite of the appalling number of dead, exceeding a million, the Americans nevertheless, in spite of all this, are trying once more to repeat this dreadful slaughter. It seems that the long blockade following after a fierce war, the dismemberment and the destruction are not enough for them. So they come again today to destroy what remains of this people and to humiliate their Muslim neighbors.

While the purpose of the Americans in these wars are religious and economic, they also serve that petty state of the Jews, to divert attention from their occupation of Jerusalem and their killing of Muslims in it.

There is no better proof of all this than their eagerness to destroy Iraq, the strongest of the neighboring Arab states, and their attempt to dismember all the states of the region, such as Iraq and Saudi Arabia and Egypt and Sudan, into petty states, whose division and weakness would ensure the survival of Israel and the continuation of the calamitous Crusader occupation of the lands of Arabia (Lewis, 2003).

Bin Laden affirmed in the above statement that the American presence in the Arabia land is a war against Muslims that requires unequivocal cooperation of all Muslims to Jihad movement to declare war against Americans and those who support their ideas. Bin Laden's statement does not only intend to ostracize contemporary Muslims who have conceived democratic philosophy, but to orchestrate catastrophic division in the world where the Islam faith would appear to be on the opposing side of societal harmony.

To recall history, individuals have been observed to be willing to gradually modify culture and other mores. But faith based tradition or values have been slow to develop. If the idea of keeping religious values is dogmatic, irreconcilable, and irreversible than, there should be a theory that would explain with corroborative evidence the irreversibility of the religious philosophy that has cocooned individuals to certain religious creeds. Individuals are more likely to clench to an idea if that idea is supernaturally utopia and each believer of the idea perceived themselves to have direct personal gain and interest. One theory that could explain the Islamic military/extremism or Jihad crescendo is based on the ideology that those that fight or died in the name of Islam will have place in paradise automatically (Bostom, 2005 & Fregosi, 1998). The belief that fighting, killing or dying in the name of Islam has become labyrinthine to an extent that the militants are taking pleasure in death rather than being victorious living heroes. This convoluted religious belief of killing and dying in the name of Allah was theorized by Fregosi in his book Jihad. Fregosi explained that "even more than Allah, the prime motive for fighting that inspired the Arabs were plunder, slaves, women, and eagerness for death fighting for Islam"(Fregosi, 1998, p. 66). With the understanding of this theory, it can be validated that individuals can clench to certain inflexible religious doctrine not only for the purpose of serving God, but the effort of religious commitment is being complemented by their envisaged personal gains and gratifications.

THE BIG QUESTION

The question remained is, why have some group of individuals indulged certain religious creed such as obligation to serve God to endanger other's life? How can the pursuit of democracy peacefully modify and transform the divisive religious creeds in an effort to create a negotiated balance or common golden thread that would be the catalyst for world mutual interaction? In order to respond to these critical inquires; we must first have in-depth understanding of the hypnotized ideology that tends to remote control the believers of negative religious ethos that created a state of paranoia among our kind. In a rational framework, one would think that the purpose of religion is to exult God's omnipotence and edify those that believe in him. However, the notion that individuals that are yet to accept Islam's principles are enemies to God; therefore, they should be forced to repent or they would be exterminated does not exemplify the Islamic religious Arabic greetings: (*salaamu alaikum*) peace be with you and (*Allahu Akbar*) God is great (Schwartz, 2002).

It is understood that God created the entire universe within six days without galvanizing support of any kind from humankind; therefore, it would be difficult for out group (non Muslims) to conform to the Islamic doctrine that encourages militancy for God in an effort to kill those who do not accept him as a most high. It is also obvious to believe that with the clairvoyant power of God, he has the ability to crunch anyone who antagonizes his supremacy. God is omnipresence and knows who his true worshipers are. The idea of being foot soldiers for God and a sense of enhancing a universal religion through military hegemony is the major foundation for Jihad and Islamic extremism. The Jihad in the holy Qur'an is written as follows:

> *9.5: But when the forbidden months are past, then fight and slay the pagans wherever ye find them, and seize them, beleaguer them, and lie in whit for them in every stratagem (of war); but if they repent (accept Islam) and establish regular prayers and practices regular charity than open the way for them; God is oft-forgiving, Most Merciful.*

> *9.29: fight those who believe not in Allah nor the last day, nor hold that forbidden which hath been forbidden by Allah and his apostle, nor acknowledge the religion of truth even if they are the people of the book, until they pay the Jizya with willing submission, and feel themselves subdued.*

> *9.73: O Prophet! Strive against the disbelievers and the hypocrites! Be harsh with them. Their ultimate abode is hell, a hapless journey's end.*

> *9.111: Allah hath purchased of the believers their persons and their goods; for theirs (in turn) is the garden (of paradise); they fight in His cause, and slay and are slain; a promise biding on Him in truth, through the law, the Gospel, and the Qur'an, and who is more faith to his covenant than*

Allah? Then rejoice in the bargain which ye have concluded: that is the achievement supreme.

9.123: O ye who believe! Fight those of the disbelievers who are near to you, and let them find harshness in you, and know that Allah is with those who keep their duty (unto Him).

4.74: Let those fight in the cause of Allah who sell the life of this world for the hereafter. To him who fighteth in the cause of Allah – whether he is slain or gets victory – soon shall we give him a reward of great (Value).

4.76: Those who believe fight in the cause of Allah, and those who reject faith fight in the case of Evil: so fight ye against the friends of Satan: feeble indeed is the cunning of Satan.

4.95: O ye who believe! Shall I show you a commerce that will save you from a painful doom? You should believe in Allah and His messenger, and should strive for the cause of Allah with your wealth and your lives. That is better for you, if ye did but know... Allah hath granted a grade higher to those who strive and fight with their goods and persons than those who sit (at home).

2.216: Fighting is prescribed for you, and ye dislike it. But it is possible that ye dislike a thing which is good for you, and that ye love a thing which is bad for you. But Allah knoweth, and ye know not.

2.217: They ask thee concerning fighting in the Prohibited Month. Say: "fighting therein is a grave (offense); but graver is it in the sight of Allah to prevent access to the path of Allah, to deny Him, to prevent access to the Sacred Mosque, and drive out its members." Tumult and oppression are worse than slaughter. Nor will they cease fighting you until they turn you back from your faith if they can. And if any of you Turn back from their faith and die in unbelief, their works will bear no fruit in this life and in the Hereafter; they will be companions of the fire and will abide therein.

2.218: Those who believed and those who suffered exile and fought (and strove and struggled) in the path of Allah;-they have the hope of the Mercy of Allah: And Allah is Oft-forgiving, most Merciful.

2.191: And slay them wherever ye catch them, and turn them out from where they have turned you out... such is the reward of those who suppress faith.

8.12: ... "I will instill terror into the hearts of the unbelievers: smite ye above their necks and smite all their finger-tips of them."

8.15, 16: O ye who believe! When ye meet the unbelievers in hostile array, never turn your backs to them. If any do turn his back to them on such a day-unless it be in a stratagem of war, or to retreat to a troop (of his own) – he draws on himself the wrath of Allah, and his abode is Hell – an evil refuge (indeed)!

8.39: And fight them on until there is no more tumult or oppression, and there prevail justice and faith in Allah altogether and everywhere; but if they cease, verily Allah doth see all that they do.

8.41: And know that out of all the booty that ye may acquire (in war), a fifth share is assigned to Allah,-and to the Messenger, and to near relatives, orphans, the needy, and the wayfarer,-if ye do believe in Allah and in the revelation We sent down to Our Servant on the Day of Testing – the Day of the meeting of the two forces. For Allah hath power over all things.

8.65: O Apostle! **Rouse** *the believers to the fight; if there are twenty amongst you, patient and persevering, they will vanquish two hundred; if a hundred, they will vanquish a thousand of the unbelievers; for these are a people without understanding.*

48.20: …Allah promises you much booty (spoils of war) that you will capture from the defeated infidels… (Bostom, 2005).

The portion of the Qur`an "Jihad" is very astonishing to the extent that it not only provokes disunity among people of Islam and other religions, but it establishes principles that were so-called mandated by God. This explanation does not suggest that Jihad is not of God or an instruction from Prophet Muhammad. It is common sense that if Muhammad truly received these instructions from God, it would be worthwhile to vividly understand the context of the event at the time God gave these instructions to Muhammad. When Muhammad introduced the monotheistic philosophy, it was a birth of a new religion or ideology that came under violent criticism by the Mecca Quraysh tribe, where he originated. This tribe was considered the master of the idolatry tradition of the Middle Eastern region. Was the Jihad not a timeline instruction for Muhammad to vanquish the idolaters of the Quraysh tribe that distasted the prophet's revelation regarding one God that has power above all gods? Was the Jihad not intended for the enemies of Prophet Muhammad who denied the prophet's divine revelation on grounds that accepting a newer religion would disperse them from worshiping their gods or idols and taking away financial and other benefits being gained from their annual idolatry pilgrimages?

QURAN, JIHAD, AND TIME

There is no doubt that Islam is a legitimate religion that has gained prominence around the world. It is also acknowledged that Islamic Jihad has some fundamental religious values that are acceptable by other religions and the society as a whole. For example, Jihad in a positive Islamic interpretation relates to charity work and being goodwill ambassador for

God. David Dakake defines Jihad in Lumbard's book as the ability of individuals to go beyond the confines of their ego and desires-or anything that ones bears with or strive after for the sake of pleasing God are considered as Jihad(Lumbard, 2004). Dakake further stated in his personal insight about Jihad that "Jihad also requires individuals immeasurable exertion of oneself for the sake of God in ways such as controlling one's self and showing patience and forgiveness in the face of offense, to gaining authentic knowledge, to physical fighting to stop oppression and injustices" (Lumbard, 2004:3). With Dakake's interpretation of the Jihad relative to the doctrinal teaching of Qur'an, it is crucial that we further examining some teachings of the Qur'an that contradict the peaceful aspects of Jihad. Section 8 of the Holy Qur'an talks about Muslims' relationship with non Muslims. The Qur'an states in this section that "O you who believe, take not the Jews and the Christians friends-they are friends of each other- and whoever among you takes them for friends he is indeed one of them- surely Allah guides not the unjust (5:51). O you who believe, take not for friends those who take your religion as a mockery and a sport, from among those who were given the book before you and the disbelievers; and keep your duty to Allah if you are believers (5:57).

In an effort to understanding these two Quranic teachings, we first must look at how the Muslim world has related to the Jews and Christians in the past and the current status of their relationship. It is not our responsibility to provide meaning other than what is provided; however, the readers will use their intelligence to give unbiased interpretation to these Quranic verses. While we are not giving meaning to (5:51) of the Qur'an, it would also create controversy if others would interpret this verse and say that it does not seed the current dispute among the three religious groups. What needed to be explored is that, do these two scriptural teachings above remain or appear to be the precipitating factors for the genesis of the current dispute between the Jews and Christians on one hand and Muslims on the other hand? One might argue that these scriptures did not specifically mention Christians and Jews being adversaries to Muslims; it is a common sense to conclude that if and individual is considered not a friend, there are two things that come to mind; isolating or vanquishing the individual. If the Qur'an declares both Christians and Jews not friends to Muslims; who are they to the Muslims? What was the intended purpose of this teaching?

These two verses continue to be the seeds for the dispute between the Muslims on one hand and Jews and Christians on the other hand. Another important point Dakake discussed about his insight in (5:51) of the Qur`an is that this verse was revealed to one of the earlier Islam prophets during the battle of Badr in 623 C.E or around the battle of Uhud in 625 C. E (Lumbard, 2004). Dakake further noted that the intended purpose for this verse was to keep unity among the than young growing Muslim community to work together and overcome the idolaters or the Maccans who opposed the birth of Islam. One thing that needs to be clear is that the battles of Badr and Uhud were not between Jews and Muslims or was it between Christians and Muslims. The dispute was amongst Arab Muslims and non Muslim Arabs who opposed Islam.

Alluding to ideas, religious philosophy, or tradition such as the Islamic Jihad that existed almost one thousand three hundred and eight six years ago is a mere idea of converting contemporary civilization to prehistoric civilization where humankind was barbaric in their interaction and hunting and gathering were major life phenomenon. There are provisions in the Qur`an, Jihad that are astonishing to an extent that they do not only provoke disunity between Islam and people of different religion, but they validate the so-called mandate from Allah that instructed Muslims to forcefully convert non Muslims to Muslim or they should be killed by Muslims (Bostom,2005, & Peter, 1994). To disagree with certain portions of Jihad does not necessarily suggest that it is not divine or that it was not instructed by Prophet Muhammad. If Muhammad truly received these instructions from Allah as claimed by Muslim extremists, wise minds would inquire for whom these laws were intended. Were they intended for Muhammad to use them as instruments to vanquish the idolaters in the Arabian area or people from his hometown of Mecca who detested his monotheistic philosophy they perceived to be an idea that would divorce them from worshiping their gods or idols? Was the Jihad not intended for the enemies who denounced Muhammad's divine revelation on grounds that accepting newer religion would dispose them from worshiping their idols; thus taking away financial and other benefits being gained from their annual pilgrimages? Was Jihad not intended for the era in which the Islam religion was born? These questions are fundamental inquires that require depth and precise respond to insight critical thinkers regarding the application of Jihad philosophy to contemporary society.

It sometimes appears unparallel to discuss religion and evolution simultaneously; however, it is equally necessary to find the contiguity of the two ideas and see the reality from each end that continues to impact human existence.

Evolutionists and creationists could not be in the same paragraph; however, creationists might agree with the development of human activities over time period with regards to technology. For example, before modern days technology, Paleolithic tools such as the Levalloisian Technique was used for coal preparation; the Disk Coal technique also used for coal shaping; stone age tools, Bronze Age where tools were made by men from the melting and mixing of Bronze and Tin; cave men tools such as Blade-used to prepare food for cooking; scraper used to skin animals; Pumice stone used to smooth tools made; antler or wood; Harpoon Head used for hunting and fishing; Limpet Scoop used to limpet from Shell; Mattock used to striping meat and also used for digging roots; pebble tools; stone flake used as knives were common for human domestic consumption (Zimmer, 2005, Sullivan, 1980, & Peregrine, 2003).

Before present-day technology, humans invented tools out of wood, stones, bronze etc. by making use of their immediate environment. Today, these stones, middle, Paleolithic, and Neolithic age tools are not used; however, if these tools still are being manufactured and used, they are not in the same form or shape. If these changes are cogent evidence, what would it means to the Muslim extremists regarding the Quranic Jihad? Will it be rational to say that as the early days tools were made to satisfy the desire of the people, it is as the same as the Jihad in the Qur`an – the Jihad was given to Muhammad to overcome the Quraysh or present-day Maccans who detested the gospel of Prophet Muhammad? Or, will it be rational to suggest that civilization of yesterday was not intended to control the today's era? While the theory of creation has not been accepted to run parallel with the theory of evolution, it might be obvious to accept that the discussion of development is necessary in our religious doctrines in an effort for our beliefs to be consistent with our civilization.

The analogy with early tools and the Jihad could be understood; however, the battle of Badr between Muhammad and his followers on one hand and the idolaters on the other hand was fought with spear, bowls, and arrows, while foot solders moved or traveled on horses; present day Muslim extremists are not fighting with these same weapons. Why? They are not fighting with those weapons because technology has evolved or developed and are mutual with present day civilization. Today, the Jihad is using AK-47, rocket-propelled grenades (RPG), M-203, and BAR machineguns etc., to fight for what they believe to be truth. What would this technological development mean to the Jihad movement? If the Jihad movement accepts using products of the technology revolution weaponry, it would be wise for them to accept the evolution of religious doctrine such as Jihad; thereby, redefine the basic principle of Islam: Obligation, arbitration, and mediation to be consistent with present day civilization. Until Jihad and the three words (obligation, arbitration, and mediation) that are considered to be the fundamental principle of the Islamic religion are redefined in the context of creating a cohesive, vibrant, and civilized society, it would be difficult for democracy to reach its pinnacle of success in the world. The Jihad was given to Muhammad as a tool to gain spiritual hegemony over the idolaters of Mecca who detested his monotheistic philosophy. The idea of Jihad was not written where it is not subject to modification, change, or development. The refusal by Islam believers to modernize their doctrine to agree with current societal norms will continue to deter the enhancement of democracy around the world especially, in the Middle Eastern region.

One idea that is certain among Christians is the disagreement with evolutionary theory; however, Christian theologians or historians have written the evolved version of the Holy Bible, (The New Testament). The New Testament repudiates some of the Old Testament teachings or accounts of Prophet Moses that state:

> *If men strive, and hurt a woman with child, so that her fruit depart from her, and yet no mischief follow: he shell be surely punished, according as the woman's husband will lay upon him; and he shall pay as the judges determine.*

> *And if any mischief follow, then thou shalt give life for life, eye for eye, tooth for tooth, hand for hand, foot for foot, burning for burning, wound for wound, stripe for stripe (The Holy Bible: Exodus 21:22-25)*

The above biblical provision encouraged war and other forms of violence such as Jihad in the Holy Qur`an. For example, the Old Testament stated that he who killed any man; he shall be killed; while the version of the New Testament that modified the Old Testament's eye for an eye sates:

> Ye have heard that it hath been said, An eye for an eye, and a tooth for a tooth; But I say unto you, That ye resist not evil: but whosoever shall smite thee on thy right cheek, turn to him the other also...(The Holy Bible: St. Matthew 5:38-39).

Throughout Jesus' teaching in the Bible, he modified all the teachings of old that encouraged vengeance, acquisitive, retaliation and other ideologies of violence. Another interesting account of the New Testament is when Jesus' disciple, Simon Peter decided to fight for him and cuts one of the servants of the High Priest, Malchus' ears. Jesus denounced Peter's action and told him: "put up thy sword into the sheath: the coup which my father hath given me, shall I not drink it" (The Holy Bible: St. John 18:11)?

What does Jesus' action of placing Malchus's ear back and his statement of drinking out of the cup his father gave him mean? Jesus was denouncing vengeance and teaching tolerance, thereby, rejecting Mosaic teaching of an eye for an eye or a tooth for a tooth. Jesus' teaching does not indicate that Moses' teachings and laws were not from God; Jesus acknowledged that Moses' doctrines were from God and were appropriate for the context of the era or period of time in which he (Moses) lived and taught. Jesus also acknowledged that the vengeance doctrine of Moses was an outcome of the hundreds of years Israelites were oppressed. In such context, if God had stressed equal emphasis on tolerance and revenge, Moses and his people could have remained in captivity and lost their dignity. As a result of the long period of oppression afflicted on the Israelites, God authorized tough retaliation during that time period. Until the birth of Jesus' era, the Jews were accustomed to the culture of vengeance and retaliation.

Even the Holy Qur'an states "Then your hearts hardened after that, (the oppression or subjugation) so that they were like rocks, rather worse in hardness. And surely there are some rocks from which streams burst forth; and there are some of them which split asunder some water flows from them; and there are some of them which fall down for the fear of

Allah; and Allah is not heedless of what you do" (Qur'an 2:74). It is understood from this passage that God himself directed Moses with instructions of revenge due to the time period and the context of their affliction. One could also argue that the Qur'an teaches tolerance; however, to what extent the Muslim extremists are practicing the Quranic teaching that states "And the recompense of evil is punishment like it; but whoever forgives and amends, his reward is with Allah; surely He loves not the wrong doers; and whoever is patient and forgives- that surely is an affair of great resolution" (Qur'an 42: 40 & 43). The key word in this teaching is forgiveness, and not retribution or any form of reprisal.

The New Testament Holy Bible is the evolved version of the Old Testament. Unfortunately, there has not been any newer version of the Holy Qur'an that would modify its doctrines such as Jihad to be in agreement with present-day civilization.

The prospect of democracy in the Muslim world will continue to be at a slower or difficult pace until the torchbarriers of the philosophy (democracy) embark or negotiate with contemporary Muslims to redefine the fundamental principles of the religion and inspire a newer version of the Holy Qur'an.

The question that comes to mind when suggesting the rewriting of the Holy Qur'an is: what is the possibility of Muslims accepting the reproduction of their holy book? The journey to rewriting the Qur'an will be difficult to achieve, but its product will be vibrant cohesive society building. It will be a war that cannot be won with weapons of destruction. This will be a psychological war that would be won with intelligence and well crafted and supported philosophy.

For example, when Adolf Hitler took leadership of Nazi Germany, he introduced an idea that helped to perpetuate his regime for twelve years. Hitler, as head of the German Socialist Party, wanted to control the whole of Germany. He said in most of his public speeches that "He alone who owns the youth gains the future" (Keeley, 1974, p. 10). The German Socialist Party introduced an idea that created a youth formation called Youth for Hitler, an idea intended to bring eligible boys and girls under Nazi's control. The process culminated with legislation in 1936 making it mandatory for every eligible youth between ages 10 and 18 to automatically become a member of Hitler's Youth Formation (Keeley, 1974). Hitler invested in the youth group; they were trained to be physically strong and mentally tough; they were immediately enlisted in the Germany Army to implement Hitler's ideas as soon as they matured in the youth group. Hitler's philosophy of he who owns the youth gains the future was vindicated with his investment in the German youth that resulted in cementing his power for twelve years with unflinching loyalty from the young military.

This youth analogy does not suggest any replica of Hitler's dictatorial doctrine; however, it suggests that in order for democracy to succeed, its torchbearers should invest in the education of Muslim youth with contemporary cohesive societal building ideologies that would modify religious doctrine such as military Jihad and, at the same time, helping them keep the socially acceptable values or beliefs of the Holy Qur'an. Thereby, Islamic extremists would practice the verse in Qur'an that states: and not alike are the good and the evil. Repel (evil) with what is best, when lo! He between whom and thee is enmity would be as if he were a warm friend. And none is granted it but those who are patient, and none is granted it but the owner of a might good fortune (Qur'an 41:34–35).

Chapter 3
Democracy in the Eye of Hinduism

BRIEF REVIEW AND INSIGHT IN HINDUISM

Unlike Judaism, Islam, Christianity etc., which believe in a monotheistic philosophy of worship, Hinduism is on the other side of the religious spectrum – it believes in a multiplicity of gods.

Democracy in the context of Hinduism is difficult and critical to discuss due to the religion, almost lack of antique written historical record. Most history of Hinduism prior to recent history that would date as recent as 1500 BCE where all forms of myth, legend or some forms of invalidated beliefs. For example, the birth of Islam came through the revelation of God through Prophet Muhammad with specific instruction in an identified historical time period; the birth of Judaism was established on the biblical principle of the Old Testament that has chronological historical prophets data and events; Christianity emerged in an identified historical time period that begun with Jesus Christ, just to name a few. Hinduism, on the other hand emerged as a belief of the mind based on speculation that was not recorded to answer question such as when, how, where, what, and why. Based on the oral historical nature of Hinduism, it is almost difficult for the outside group to comprehend the dynamics of the religion. However, the tradition and culture of the religion being observed in our contemporary society has suggested that it is not only a religion, but a way of life that predicts its believers' characters and their perception of democracy.

In order to validate the notion that Hindus characters are direct product of their religion, it is important to outlook some of their religious orientation principles or philosophies and at the same time gain insight in the emergence of the religion. What is recently recorded as foundation of Hinduism derived from a belief system that states, prior to the existence of Prophet Moses and Jesus Christ other wise men had lived and allegedly stood on India's river banks and sang. The alleged songs were very pleasant and melodious to an extent that the Hindus believes that the songs or voices where not of ordinary men, but inspired by some supernatural power. The Hindus conceived, henceforth, that out of the inspired melodies of the songs over 15,000 stanzas were collected. The collected stanzas were passed down as oral tradition and based on the belief that the songs were characterized by supernatural power; the love of the songs then eventually became culture of the Hindus and later emerged as religion (Hinduism). Since the emergence of this musical faith, it has inspired over three hundred million people in India and about fifteen million people around the world.

HINDUS' RELIGIOUS WORLDVIEW AND DEMOCRACY

Hinduism believes strongly in extraterrestrial power as other religions do; however, one uncertainty that continues to doubt others is the incarnation characteristics of their one god (Brahman) into about three hundred and thirty million gods. The incarnation of Brahman creates a situation where almost every family in the Hindu society has the liberty to choose certain aspects of the three hundred and thirty million incarnation of Brahman they wish to worship. The characteristics of Brahman continue to develop controversy among Hindu philosophers and the world on the other hand. With the almost countless gods of the religion, contemporary Hindus assert that they worship one god with infinite aspects, while some Hindus accept the gods as individual bodies. Based on the infinite characteristics of the Brahman the Hindus believe in a theory that validates the unbounded nature of their god. They believe in the eternal recurrence of life. For example, there is an indoctrinated notion that the life of a caterpillar ends, but reappears as butterfly, the butterfly dies, but it eggs hatch and later there are more caterpillars; an idea that is supported by scientific theory that states: matter is never destroy, but changes from one form to another (Luce, 1968). With the knowledge of the infinite characteristics of life, the Hindus conceives that even living things such as trees can change form to animals, from animal to human and from one human body to another; an argument that could be in the same paragraph with Charles Darwin's theory of evolution that holds the notion that all life are related an descended from a common ancestor and developed into another form. Hence, the Hindus knowledge about life has invisible or infinite source.

The multiple characteristics of Brahman, the Hindus' God, and the circular notion of life brings all Hindus irrespective of which Brahman they worship to a universal Hindu-defined philosophy: purity, self-control, detachment, truth, nonviolence, charity and an unflinching sympathy toward all creatures. The uncompromised compassion of the religion toward all creatures is taught as a code of ethics and values across the Hindu world. The Manu-in Hindu that is considered the founder of humankind and the Hindu lawgiver teaches:

> *Wound not others do no one injury by thought or by deed, utter no word to pain thy fellow creatures. He who habitually salutes and constantly pays reverence to the age obtains an increase of four things: length of life, knowledge, fame and strength...Depend not on another, but lean instead on thyself. True happiness is born of self reliance... By falsehood a sacrifice becomes vain; by self-complacency the reward for austerities is lost; by boasting the goodness of an offering is brought to naught (Luce et al., 1968, p. 25).*

Before bringing Hinduism parallel to democracy, let us identify what has been recognized from our discussion of the value of Hinduism that might evoke the spirit of Democracy in the religion. At this point it should be understood that the Hindus religion's nature of worship that does not obligate the believers to monotheistic philosophy; hence, allowing them to choose from the array of gods with different powers and forces, and at the same time living together as one people, is a sense of tolerance; the nature of the religion relative to almost each family having the liberty to choose its own gods to worship is also a sense of freedom that are crucial in the concept of democracy.

While there are several gods being worshiped in Hinduism, there are three aspects of the supreme god, Brahman that are worshipped dominantly in the Hindu world based on individuals' desire: the Vishnu, a god that is concern with the preservation of creation and righteousness; the Shiva, a god of destruction in a constant process of change, and Brahma; a god of creation. If these three aspects of Brahman are understood in the context of how they impact their believers individually or collectively, one will gain insight on how the Hindus world responds to the quest of democracy.

Since religion, culture, and tradition continue to play a pivotal role in predicting individual's character, it is vital to evaluate the three major manifestation of the supreme Hindu Brahman (Vishnu, Shiva, and Brahma). In Hindu teaching, the followers of the Vishnu god consider it as god of love and it was incarnated to Rama and Krishna who came to the world as human beings to overcome evil; the Hindus that devote themselves to Shiva, an aspect of Brahman, are deeply interested in knowledge and self-discipline and acknowledge that their gods' power is not only destructive but escapes the old to make room for the new, hence, a god of neologism and possibility in Hindu teaching; and the Hindus who worship the Brahma believe that as a god of creation, he controls the universe and should be respected; however among the Hindus, those who worship Brahma are considered primitive, based on the notion that since Brahma completed the creation of the universe, he no longer is active and has no major significance (Hay, 2006) in contemporary society. The several aspects of the Hindus' supreme god that emphasize individuals' enhancing a better life is crucial to building a civilized social environment.

One question that might be obvious is: how can Hinduism be in the same conversation with democracy. The answer is simple and obvious, based on evidence that is implied in the doctrine of the religion. The doctrine or law of the Hindu religion and how it orients its believers and the believers' pronounced devotion to the faith determine their response to democracy. Manu, the religious ethics or laws of Hindus, teaches unequivocal philosophy of the Hindu religion that devotes orienting the mind of its believers to values such as diversity, as it is exemplified by the characteristics of the gods they worship; tolerance, as is obvious among the Hindus despite the multiplicity of gods and patterns of worship they practice; liberation and freedom of the Hindus as it relates to individuals having the independent faculty to choose from the various aspects of the supreme Brahman as he or she wants to worship and the caste they want to belong to, and the teaching of their holy scripture (Upanishads) of non-violence, an idea that inspired Gandhi's reformation mission in India (Klostermaier, 1998, and Hay, 2006).

BEHAVIORAL THEORIES AND HINDUS' RESPONSE TO DEMOCRACY

It is easy to understand that human behaviors are indistinguishable from their social environment. For example, Social Learning Theory, which first was espoused by Gabriel Trade (1843–1904), suggested that human behaviors develop through four main strata of imitation: close contact, imitation of superiors, understanding of concepts in a particular context, and role model behavior, thus consisting of three related aspects: observing, imitating, and reinforcement. This theory later was replicated by Julian Rotter, who suggested that the result of behavior has an impact on the urge of the individual to engage in that behavior, and also states that individuals might avoid negative consequence as they desire positive outcomes. Further, Albert Bandura expanded the theory by combining both Social Learning and Psychoanalysis theories and outlined three major patterns that predicate individuals' behaviors: retention of what an individual observed; reproduction of the observed behavior, and motivation or reason to make that behavior part of oneself (Rotter, 1954, and Bandura, 1977). The scholarly insights of Rotter and Bandura regarding the prediction of individuals' character can be discussed in the same paragraph with the impact religion has on individuals, especially the Hindus and how they respond to the quest for democracy.

How do the Hindus respond to the quest of democracy? In order to get insight of the manner in which the psychological theory of Bandura and Rotter that are said to shape or mode human behaviors, and democratic principles have some synonyms with Hinduism, it is crucial to dissect the different religious philosophical principles that appear to be the corner stones for the Hindu religion. Hinduism, despite of its numerous aspects of its Brahman (Supreme God), it has four major ideologies that orientate the Hindus: Dharma is a celestial principle of the religion that restricts the Brahman worshipers to righteousness, wholesome conducts, righteous responsibilities or duties and to sustain and behold both social and extraterrestrial harmony; the Artha is associated with the acquiring of desirable material wealth that are satisfy through adhering to the teaching of Dharma which is the religious duty of Hindus; the Kama is the philosophy of sensual love among the Hindus for one another that is also regulated by the religious duty of the religion (Dharma); and Moksha, an ideology that concludes the Hindus religious goals and releases all souls from the cycle of rebirth, and is usually considered as liberation that is predicated on the chronological achievement of all other religious philosophies, thereby resulting in freedom from all suffering and thus inheriting the enjoyment of the qualities of the Supreme Brahman (Geaves, 2006).

Besides these four cornerstones of the religion, the Karma is another doctrine of Hinduism that teaches about human activities and their consequences. The Karma teaches that the accumulated activities of an individual's life amount to the consequences and thereby predicts the reincarnation or life after death on the individual. Based on the Karma and the four corner stones of the religion, they indoctrinate their children in a way that would be coherent with Dharma, a religious duty of attaining social and celestial harmony. The socialization process of Hindus that is geared towards attaining societal harmony begins with the orientation in the metaphysics of the religion that relates to self control through physical activities such as yoga. Yoga in Hinduism is the discipline of the mind and body that is considered a crucial path to Brahman. Yoga has four major stages with discrete purposes: the Karma Yoga is considered as one of the greatest path to Brahman that is achieved through selfless action or not being attached to the fruit of action; the Jnana Yoga is concern with developing methods to achieve the intuitive knowledge of the absolute Brahman; the Bhakti Yoga is considered as the path to loving devotion and it is the way to achieve pure love for God; it introduces the idea of loving service to a personal lord who bestows his grace on human beings and allows the possibility of a close bond of love between the human and the divine; and the Raja Yoga is considered as the path of self control performed to comprehend reality or the self through direct experience and meditation (Flood,1996 and Geaves,2006).

The young Hindus are devoted to learning the religious wisdom of their religion and being indoctrinated in to the faith through Yoga. Before a Hindu child goes through the process called Twice Born, he has to complete the teaching in Yoga and becomes a true yogi. Being a true yogi has great significance to the Hindus: this means that the individual has the discipline of mind, control of the body and in the right path of performing his religious responsibilities that includes attaining social and celestial harmony. The Yoga culture of Hinduism can be summarized as means that all Hindus learn about terrestrial and celestial morals and tolerance.

The agreement between Bandura and Rotter's theory of behavior and the pillars of democracy on one hand and Hinduism on the other is the crystal religious philosophies of the Hindus that foster attaining social harmony; the diversified characteristics of the religion and multiple paths to the one God appeared synonymous to the pillars of democracy. Hinduism also tolerates other religions despite some being monotheistic and Hinduism being Zoroastrianism. In Ramakrishna, one of Hindus' priests teachings; he looked at Islam and Christianity version of worshiping God and received visions on Muhammad and Jesus that all the true religions can lead to God if they follow the righteous path. In one of his popular teachings he says:

> *You see many stars at night in the sky but find them not when the sun rises; can you say that there are no stars in the heaven of day? So, O man! Because you behold not God in the days of your ignorance, say not that there is no god. As one and the same material, water, is called by different names by different peoples, one calling it water, another calling it eau, a third aqua, and another pani, so the one Sat-chit-ananda, the everlasting-intelligent-bliss, is invoked by some as God, by same as Allah, by some as Jehovah, by some as Hari, and by others as Brahman. As one can ascend to the top of a house by means of a ladder or a bamboo or a staircase or a rope, so divers are the ways and means to approach God, and every religion in the world shows one of these ways. Different creeds are by different path to reach the Almighty...*

> *Men weep rivers of tears because a son is not born to them; others wear away their hearts with sorrow because they cannot get riches. But how many... weep and sorrow because they have not seen God? He finds who seeks Him; he who with intense longing weeps for God has found God. Truly, I say unto thee, he who longs for Him finds Him. Go and verify this in thine own life; try for three consecutive days with genuine earnestness and thou art sure to succeed...*

> *As many have merely heard of snow but not seen it, so many are the religious preachers who have read only in books about the attributes of God; and as many have seen but not tasted it, so many are the religious teachers who have got*

only a glimpse of the divine glory, but have not understood
its real essence. He...alone can describe God who has associated with Him in His different aspects, now as servant
of God, or as being absorbed in Him... The sunlight is one
and the same wherever it falls, but only bright surfaces like
water, mirrors and polished metals can reflect it fully. So is
the divine light. It falls equally and impartially on all hearts,
but only the pure and clean hearts of the good and holy can
fully reflect it (Luce et al, 1968, p.43).

The several social, cultural, and religious opulences of the Hindus
being discussed does not suggest that Hinduism has had a smooth path
in history and it is the paragon of democracy. It is not by any means suggested that the Hindus are obsequious to their neighbors in acknowledging Human Rights and democracy to its fullest. History recorded the
continues bloodshed in Kashmir, a rift between Pakistan-Indian relation
that began with Islamic invasion in the 600s; the 1906 division between
India Muslim and the Hindus in the India National Congress that resulted to the formation of the League of Muslim; the 1905 through 1911
dispute between Hindus and Muslim that resulted to the British parti-
tioning the region between Muslim Indians and Hindus Indians; Hindus
Indians entering a war between Bangladesh and Pakistan in support of
Bangladesh to free itself from Pakistan etc.

HISTORY AND RELIGIOUS UPHEAVALS
IN THE MIDDLE EAST

Prior to present day Indian popular religion, which is considered
in contemporary history as the oldest religion, there had been several
historical periods and events such as: prehistory and the Hindu Valley
civilization that could be dated as far as 6500 B.C.E. to 1500 B.C.E; a
period of agriculture on the west of the Indus River; the emergence of
the pastoral nomad society in the Deccan and the emergence of urban
societies on the Indus River; the Vedic period that started 1500 B.C.E.
and ended 800 B.C.E., a period characterized the migration of the Indo-
Aryan into northwest India, the composition of the hymns of the Rigveda,
Indo-Aryan migration eastward across north India, emergence of urban
society along Ganges River; the Epic period that characterized the inva-

sion of northwest India by Alexander the Great from 327–325 B.C.E; the popular Medieval period that characterized Arab Muslims invading northwest India 711–715 C.E. (Luce et al., 1968, & Flood,1996).

These historical periods mentioned and others untouched events were eras that the Indians came across several changes and introduction of other conqueror's civilizations and beliefs. The experiences of the Indians from foreign invaders left several peculiar indelible impacts on Indian culture, beliefs, traditions, and religion. The different stages of history gave the Hindu religion evolutionary characteristics. Hinduism is not a creedal religion that its doctrines and philosophies are dogmatic or indoctrinates its believers on absolutism. It is a religion that is open to development and evolves according to time. The open-mindedness of Hinduism gives rise to identities that are common to democracy. The pluralistic unique-ness of Hinduism begins from their theological principles that promote one God but several paths to reach him with different names for differ-ent purposes. The Hindus' democratic value of diversity is exemplified in Indian long history of religious diversity and tolerance that continue to host other religions such as Christianity, Islam, Buddhism, Judaism, Persia Zoroastrianism etc. History has also recorded and continues to record the violence in the Middle East. The uneasiness in the Middle East cannot be discussed in the absence of the regional religious ideologies that are molding religion followers' behaviors and pronouncing their responses to democracy.

The perpetuation of violence in the Middle East could be related intrinsically to the absolutism and authoritarian characteristic of Islam as history has recorded. The Islamic Jihad has multiple connotations in Arabic. In a rational sense Jihad means effort in exerting oneself; thus in Islam Jihad has been defined as exerting oneself for the sake of God in ways such as charity work, sharing with the needy, concentrating on indi-vidual prayer to have accord with God, controlling oneself by exhibiting empathy, patience and pardon in time of offenses or resentment, exploring knowledge for self benefit, physical fighting to stop subjugations, injustices etc. (Lumbard, 2004). However, the unbounded definition of Jihad has been narrowed by Islamic extremists to mean fighting for God or Holy War. The extremists' contextual definition of Jihad "Holy War" has gained prominence in the Middle East to subjugate other cultures and religions that have opposing views and dissimilar religious doctrines with Islam.

The irony of Jihad is that it disallows subjugation and domination over the Muslim world; however, the Qu`ran teaches about vanquishing and subjugating others who disbelieve in Islamism (Qu`ran 8.65). Indoctrinating the ideology of vanquishing and subjugating non Muslims give birth to Islamic absolutism and authoritarianism in the Middle Eastern region.

In a region where one of its popular religions is characterized by absolutism, the prospect of democracy is minute. It is unlikely to separate governance from religious impact when individuals that govern subscribe to religious group and the religion's philosophies channel and champions their lives; it is than obvious to say that absolutist religious environment might likely give rise to absolutist regimes and pluralistic religious environment gives rise to pluralistic regimes. Popular examples of totalitarian or absolutist regimes that might cement this argument are: the Adolf Hitler regime of Germany that perpetrated the massacre of tens of millions of Jews, Communists, Socialists, homosexuals, gypsies, and other innocents in Germany; the Romanian dictator Nicolae Ceausescu; Chilean dictator General Agusto Pinochet; absolutist Musa Traore of the west African country of Mali, who later was overthrown in a military coup by Amadou Touray; autocratic dictator Charles Taylor of the Republic of Liberia who presently is in detention in the Hague, Netherlands, facing war crimes charges; Mobuto Sese Seco, the former Zairian president; Chadian dictator Hussain Habre; Mauritanian totalitarian Maoud Ould Sid` Ahmed; former Yugoslav President Slobodan Milosevic; the former president of Uganda, Idi Amin Dada; Indonesian dictator Suharto; Lybia's Muammer Muhammad Qadhafi; former Philippines president Ferdinand Marcos; Chinese Premier Mao Zedong; absolutist Ayatollah Khomeini of Iran, etc. Pluralistic religious environments that continue to promote democracy and social justice, as well as smooth transition of government, are the United States of America, France, England, etc. With these undisputed examples, it can be suggested that the emerging and enduring democracy of India is a result of the pluralistic nature of Hinduism. There are undisputed historical accounts about Hinduism that are parallel with democracy: its doctrines and philosophies that pronounce value of life, tolerance, pluralism, diversity, and the attainment of both social and celestial harmony.

History recorded the tolerant nature of Hinduism as far as the first century when Christianity was introduced in India by St. Thomas before it gained prominence in the West and other parts of the world; the exodus of Jews to India after the Romans destroyed the Jewish temple in 70 A.D. and barred the Jewish religion; the presence of Persia's Zoroastrians in India as a result of fleeing Islamic conquest in the seventh century, etc., are facts that could fit Hinduism in the discussion of democracy.

The present coexistence of different religions in the Hindus' region could be the result of the religious orientations that divorce religious hegemony and continue to be open-minded and accepts that as diversified as the world, so are people's beliefs and faith and at the same time structure their religion with doctrines that accept to refining past doctrines in order to be mutual to present's day civilization (Flood, G. 1996). Another historical account of the Hindu religion is the intra movement for change within the religion realm that was populated by Mohandas K. Gandhi. The importance of religious orientation on human behavior was exemplified in Gandhi's struggle to gain India's independence from Britain. As discussed earlier in this chapter, the different aspects of Hinduism worship give rise to diversity of personalities and define how a follower of certain aspect of the supreme Brahman looks at life.

The two major aspects of the Brahman with diverse incarnations or manifestations that are worship are Vishnu and Shiva respectively. Gandhi was said to be the follower of Shiva, an aspect of Brahman that its followers are interested in knowledge and self discipline; with Shiva philosophical orientation, Gandhi perceived the numerous persecution, violence, and degradation the British afflicted on the Indians that included but not limited to the Amritsar massacre, the violence of Punjab that resulted in most Indian British loyalists to divorce their support from British rule and subsequently married their support to the nationalist movement from different fronts as he assumed leadership of the movement in 1920 (Walsh, 2006, and Luce et al., 1968). Gandhi responded to the British violence towards the Indian with nonviolence philosophy. After Gandhi assumed leadership of the Home Rule League, he introduced a socialistic representative democratic system where villager elected representatives to the districts, districts elected representatives to the regions and regions elected their representatives to the All-India Congress Committee; he further introduced non-cooperation of the Indians with the British rule, an idea that urge all Indians to abandon all aspects of Western business or imports (Walsh, 2006).

The idea of abandoning British industries resulted in several British aggressions against the Indians; however, it also resulted in several legislations that helped to ascend numbers of nationalist members to British governed congress. Gandhi's nonviolence protest was geared towards what her referred to as "self ruled by all legitimate and peaceful means" (Brech, 1964, 41 in Walsh, 2006, 180). One of his popular protests was the Salt March of 1930 that its significance is recorded as prelude to Indian independence.

While focus is not placed particularly on the detail history of any religion in dispensing the logic in the author's mind, the Gandhi's philosophy of nonviolence has been underscored to give insight on how individual religious orientation has profound impact on their political thoughts and behaviors. Gandhi as leader of India nationalist movement that was seeking self rule from the British, if his philosophy of seeking freedom is juxtapose with several Fatawas being issued by the Islamic movement leaders, the contrast would be robust: as broad and diverse the path to reach the supreme Hindus Brahman (God) so as were diverse nonviolence philosophies of Gandhi to gain India's independence from Britain and as autocratic or absolutist as Islam, so is its Ideology of Jihad to overcome American's rule over their so-called holy land in the Arabian Peninsula as well as subjugating those that disbelieve in the Islamic faith. Gandhi as Hindu and leader of a freedom movement made proclamations such as peaceful civil disobedience like the Salt March of 1930, boycott from civil services, boycott from buying western imported products, etc.; whereas Jihad or holy war is the only decree usually issued by Islamic so-called freedom movements to destroy people around the world including their own kind.

While Gandhi lived to see the fruit of his labor (freedom of Indians), the British created a divisive situation that continues to negatively impact the region as a whole: the division or partition of India into Hindu Indian and Muslim Indian; an idea orchestrated by Mohammad Ali Jinnah, a leader of Indian Muslim League on grounds that the nationalist movement was dominated by Hindu Indians and does not represent Muslims: Gandhi wanted a united Indian state; by November 1946 the divisiveness had clamed several lives on both sides of the Indian aisle (Indian Hindus and Indian Muslims) (Guha, 2007).

THEORETICAL EXPLANATION OF
HUMAN BEHAVIOR

The assertion in this discussion that religious orientation or socialization play key role in predicting human behavior might come under strong criticism from individuals whose religious socialization might have had negative indelible impacts on their psychology (mind), social functioning (Behavior) and political cognition (reasoning). There are several theories in both natural and social sciences that could concretize the theory of religion impacts on individuals' political reasoning. The nature versus nurture theory in natural science suggests that people behave as they do according to genetic predispositions- nature aspect of the theory; people think and behave certain ways because they are taught to do so- nurture aspect of the theory of human behavior; in Carol Dweck, one of contemporary psychologist curiosity to understand how individuals cope with failure, she developed two theories: the Fixed Mind Set theory (the believe that human qualities are carved in stone-nature) and the Growth Mind Set theory that based on the believe that individuals qualities are characters that can be cultivated through effort-nurture; Chicago school sociologists theorized that "crime was not a function of personal traits or characteristics, but rather a reaction to an environment that was inadequate for proper human relations and development"; Cesare Lombroso (1835–1909) that is known as the father of criminology derived the Biological Determinism theory of crime that suggests that violent offender had inherited or innate criminal traits that can be detected from individual's physical morphology such as cranial metrology etc. (Dweck, 2006, and Siegel, 2006: 6). The sociological theory of crime developed by Chicago School sociologists, the Lombroso Biological Determinism theory and other theories such as Conflict, Rational, Choice, Social Structure theories are all proponent on each other to validate the socialization theory of human development that states that human development and enculturation is shaped by key social process and institutions (Siegel, 2006). Henceforth, religion as a primary dominant social institution around the world is disputable that it plays no key role in modeling our persona. The argument that religion plays a major role in structuring our mind set and helps to define our persona might drive to explore the significance of paradigm shift in the society as discussed by Schriver (2004). Schriver discussed two types of paradigm shift in his book Human Behavior and the Social Environment: the Traditional Paradigm and the Alternative Paradigm (Schriver, 2006). The traditional paradigm in this context will refer to the antique ideology that perpetuates and continues to make life situation unpleasant for people just because it is their belief, and the alternative paradigm in this context will refer to the philosophy of being open-minded to accept the improvement of set beliefs with regards to the exigency of time period, places, people and the environment or other significant societal demands. Schriver discussed paradigm in the context of how human relates to their environment and defines it as: "a world view, a general perspective, a way of breaking down the complexity of the real world" (Lincoln and Guba 1985:15 in Schriver, 2006:6). Paradigm is a relation of ideas or beliefs of certain group, or it is a bunch of beliefs, values, cultures, techniques etc. shared by members of a given community. The correlation between the two types of paradigms discussed by Schriver and our discussion of religious impact of human behavior is that, religion is a set of beliefs that has its culture and traditions that individuals subscribes or behold. If this behold paradigm that might have originated from antiquity with its values that shaped the persona of people of antiquity to withstand the events and activities of that era continues to be the medium of socialization in our contemporary society without any forms of modification, change, or shift to be mutual with present days demand, that paradigm will be counterproductive. The paradigm was very essential during antiquity and thus satisfied the environment.

HUMAN BEHAVIOR, A PRODUCT OF RELIGIOUS ORIENTATION

In every religion, there is a process of socialization. Socialization in this context is a process by which new members are initiated in a lager group by means of teaching the new members the rules of the group and how it operates. The rules being indoctrinated into the new members by the old members create a world view about the group. If the rules established, for example, fifteen hundred years ago to govern people of that time period were transferred from generation to another without amendment, transformation, or any form of modification to be consistent with our evolving people and their environment, it would have the same impact it had about fifteen hundred years ago on our present-day society. In this context, since paradigms are strongly rooted in our socialization agent such as religious institutions as well a beliefs, cultures and traditions, there must be transformation of the paradigms that have the propensity to bring divisive ideology and pandemonium among human kind.

Every society has some traditions, cultural, or religious practices that are catalysts to socialize members of the religion. If the so-called socialization channel continues to be dogmatic or irreversible and refuses to shift or modify its orientation principles to be mutual with the ever evolving society, that society or group of people that subscribed to that dogmatic ideology would find it difficult to coexist with other dynamic societal worldviews.

Hinduism as a religion has come a long way from different strata or spheres of civilizations such as: the mystical revelation of the religion through sages who allegedly stood on the banks of India's river and sang; the songs allegedly had 15,000 stanzas; the Harappan civilization (2500 B.C.E) that was characterized by antique plumbing and irrigation, purification of people as Archeologist discovered a symbolic structure at Mohen-Daro call the great Bath is interpreted as evidence of the people of the Indus Valley placing emphasis on their religious practices on hygiene and ritual purification; the Indo-Aryans invasion of India that overwhelmed the original culture of Indus valley, adjacent villages and other parts of the region became nomadic or invaders cultural dominated and has up to present created a debate that Sanatana Dharama an aspect of Hindus religious worship is said to be culture of the invaders and not practices of the indigenous Indian; the Veda period (C. 1000–400 B.C) that was characterized by practices such as the immolation of widows on their husband's funeral pyres; the classical period partially under the Skanda Gupta empire (455–67 C. E.) and other civilizations have made Hinduism an icon of evolving culture (Clarke, 1993). Despite the multiplicity of the gods worshipped by Hindus, the diversified nature of their society that is predicated on different civilization periods created positive impacts on the Indian society relative to democracy. The Indians' ability to shift paradigms from civilization to another; from antique pattern of worship to contemporary divinity; and the acceptance of other religions such as Islam, Christianity, Buddhism, etc. in their culture are examples of religious tolerance and an idea of creating a pluralistic cultural, religious, and cohesive social environment.

In Dweck's (2006) Mindset theory of success, he discussed both Growth and Fixed Mindsets. These two mindsets can complement our discussion on religions to give a vivid understanding of the effect on evolved and dogmatic religious doctrines. The fixed mindset will relate to quixotic rococo religious culture that governed during antiquity that are expected to continue age after age without leaving room for modification or any form of development. This intricate mindset denounced the modernity of social development and religious tolerance. The fixed mindset creates a situation where individual or group that try to maintain their beliefs, defends and proof it right even if that belief is wrong. For example, the doctrine of Islam that teaches that the Holy Qu`ran is the completion of God's message to humankind and the termination or conclusion of previous holy revelations or teaching (Clarke, 1993). The fixed mindset that the holy Qu`ran supersedes all Holy Scriptures and concludes God's activities on earth creates a situation where others who do not subscribe to Islamic faith to investigate the validity of Islamic theology. This fixed religious mindset of Islamic supremacy over other faiths could be interpreted to mean that laws and instructions relative to vengeance, retributions etc. that God inspired Mohammad with during the origin of Islam to conquer non Muslim and pagans continues to govern our society; it may also be interpreted to mean God has terminated his activities with humankind, thereby, abandoning his creation to man for man to control the universe at his wish; it can also be interpreted to mean that other religions who will behold their faith and subscribe to the dynamics of the universe are automatic enemies to Islam and God, an interpretation that is championing Islamic teaching that legitimates the militancy interpretation of Jihad that:

> the basis of the obligation of jihad is the universality of the Muslim revelation. God's world and God's message are for all mankind; it is the duty of those who have accepted (Muslims) them to strive (jahada) unceasingly to convert or at least to subjugate those who have not (pagans and non Muslims). This obligation is without limit of time or space. It must continue until the whole world has either accepted the Islamic faith or submitted to the power of the Islamic state.

> *Until that happens, the world is divided into two: the House of Islam (dar al-Islam), where Muslims rule and the law of Islam prevails; and the House of war (dar al-harb), comprising the rest of the world. Between the two there is a morally necessary, legally and religiously obligatory state of war, until the final and inevitable triumph of Islam over unbelief (non Muslim and pagans). According to the law books, this state of war could be interrupted, when expedient, by an armistice of truce of limited duration. It could not be terminated by a peace, but only by a final victory (Bernard Lewis, in Kressel N. J. 2002:60).*

On the other hand, the Growth Mindset could help to interpret the religious beliefs that accept the evolving characteristics of the universe with regards to culture, tradition, beliefs, religion and the people that behold these societal values: it may also means that there is no absolute path to God, ideals-there are always room for compromising ideology and belief to be in agreement with the evolving nature of the universe. For example, Hinduism as the oldest religion had stratification of people in their society was referred to as the Caste Systems with four major stratifications and one substratum that labeled each stratum to a fixed social duty: the Brahmins stratum consists of the priests and philosophers, and specialists in the life of the spirit; the Kshatriys stratum consists of the nobility of feudal India (kings, warriors, and vassals) with fixed responsibility to preserve, and guide the society; the Vaishyas was traditionally made up of farmers, merchants or economic specialists also with fixed responsibility to bring economic growth in the society; the Shudra Caste consists of physical laborers and skilled craftsperson, and the least substratum of the strata consists of the untouchable (dalits) that were assigned with fixed responsibilities such as removing human wastes, corpses, sweeping streets/ janitorial services, custodians of public places, working with leather from the skins of dead cows, social duty that made individual that belongs to this caste group their bodies and clothing repugnant to others (Fisher, 2002). The previous absolutist nature of the caste society was ingrained into the social system of the Hindus until it became hereditary; a Fixed Mindset that deterred development and progress in the Indus society for years. However, Growth Mindset was introduced by social transformational figure such as Mahatma Gandhi when he attacked the injustices of the Caste system and renamed the untouchable as children of God or Harijans (Fisher, 2002). The transformation of the Caste System initiated by Gandhi has progressed to an extent that the so-called untouchables or Harijans as Gandhi labeled them have managed and have organized themselves into a powerful political group to resist the economic and social injustices they have suffered due to their schedule in the Caste system. The caste systems are being terminated because of the Hindus' society wiliness to accept the Growth Mindset philosophy for time to coin social norms or mores of their society. Beyond the impact of the Growth mindset that Gandhi had on the lower class of the caste, he also was respectful to other religions and believed that there is one God, but many different ways to reach him. Gandhi was an enthusiast of Jesus' Sermon on the Mount and thus it influenced his nonviolent campaign against British domination in India. The religious diversity of India created some fundamental changes in Hinduism. The presence of Christianity among the Hindus gave rise to Hindus reform movement that sought transformation or reformation of Hinduism in an effort to abolish the pantheon of gods and goddesses to devote worships and services directly to God himself as omnipotence (Rice, 1973). The introduction of monotheistic ideology in a popular Indian Hindu society was a phenomenon that soon slow down; however, its effects that left on Hinduism is evident in the religion institutions established by Indian missionaries in the United States and around the world; these institutions are being managed by Americans and continue to attract many young Indian Hindus; hence, culture is being modified in these institutions with the teachings, instructions, and presence of Americans and other nationals.

There is no doubt that older Hindus in the Indian villages would continue to hold the traditions of the religion; however, the young generations who have traveled abroad and attending diversified colleges and universities are more likely to acculturate. The continue changes being associated with the Hindu culture has created a paradigm shift where old religious philosophies are being diluted and thus gave chance for democracy to ooze Hindus institutions and gradually becoming a symbol of diversity and tolerance in the Middle Eastern region.

Chapter 4
Democracy in the Eye of Christianity

BRIEF OVERVIEW OF CHRISTIANITY

Religions around the world have believers, and Christianity is no exception. One thing that is certain is that if individuals would be more competent about religion before they subscribe to it, they might have a second thought. To get the full insight of religion, one should be mentally investigative and inquire with oneself about the emergence of a particular religion's purpose, derivation, and character of the initiators or torchbearers, and at most envisaging the perpetual prosperity of the religion. These crucial inquiries or religious puzzles are philosophical environments of every religion that should be revealed to individuals before being initiated.

Our discussion throughout this book is geared toward providing substantial evidence on how culture, traditions, customs, beliefs and religions as social socialization agents have impacts on the present increase of global terrorism, thereby, projecting a prescription that would manage, minimize, and control the present and future terrorist global epidemic that also is imminent. While terrorism has caused great physical damage, it is a psychological phenomenon that is deeply rooted in cultural beliefs and religious orientations.

In order to understand the culture of Christianity, it is important first to gain insight into the conception and the birth of the religion. The religion got its name from the world "Christ," a name that was given to Jesus after his resurrection and subsequent ascendance to heavenly glory. Christ is a Jewish name that is interpreted in Greek as "Messiah," and it also can be called Yeshua or Joshua, which means Yahweh, helps in Hebrew (Geaves, 2006). Christianity derived from Christ. Christ plus ians equals Christians. Christian means individual who behold the beliefs of Christ and practice the values and philosophy he inspired. What are the values and philosophies of Christ? Before we become informed about the philosophical ideology of Christ let's take the analogy of being an American. America is the root word for American and being an American means being democratic, understanding diversity, being tolerant, and being persuasive to reach your full potential. Being American means you withhold all the values of America that include but not limited to patriotism, and freedom and welfare of the people. On the other hand the values of Christ were associated with empathy, passion, diversity, tolerance and other values that promote societal cohesiveness. Most of Christ's values will be discuss in our subsequent pages.

Christianity emerged from Judaism and it is primarily behold by people who believe in the preaching and teaching of Jesus Christ. Christians are followers of Christ. In one of Christ's idiom remarks he stated that "if you love me, take my cross and follow me". Christians are therefore cross-bearers of Christ. In another words, since the analogy of being an American is to behold the values of America; we can now understand that being a Christian is to believe and practice the teachings of Christ or being a replica of his doctrine. What were than the teaching of Christ, what where his philosophies and his passion? Understanding these concepts will allow individuals to know if Christianity supports terrorism or embrace democracy.

Christianity came in the religious ream as fragment with its initial torchbearers were all Jews. However the new sect came under strong criticism by some Jewish leaders. From the origin of the Christian sect it was viewed as an intolerant religion that does not recognize any other religion's god besides its own celestial divinity; thus it was popularly considered as a religion that was refuted by prominent Jews and embraced by slaves, women and other social outcast (Cavendish, 1980). The nature of Christianity being characterized by tolerance and empathy, especially identifying with non-prominent segments of the society, was a philosophy that was condemned by Jewish leaders and its congregations usually were interrupted and disturbed by its antagonists from the Jewish community. The rejected sect soon become worldwide due to its peculiar philosophy that appeals to the majority, who were a minority segment of ancient Jews due to social stratifications. The value of Christianity that appeared to embrace the less fortunate made the religion to soon be considered a sect that has true religious characteristic. Before Christianity, there were other religious or social values that were behold by the society; however, Christianity evolved to gain prominence worldwide because of the torchbearer, Jesus cry for social decency and cohesiveness he pleaded and was dispensed through the New Testament Holy Bible. While Christianity was considered a deviant fragment of Judaism, it did not denounce the validity of the Torah or the Old Testament. Jesus validated the teaching of the Torah; however, he at the same time acknowledges that the teaching of Torah was customized according to time period by God and also believed that it was time for those laws to improve and embrace tolerance and diversity ....

Christianity did not only teach diversity and tolerance, but its viewpoints about the manifestation or reincarnation of God into man, came into the world as a savior, redeemer, reverence teacher and veneer for the sin of humankind and coupled with his philosophy of giving hope to the downthrown appealed to so many people. The monotheistic values of Christianity is visible in other religions; however, the principle of the religion that makes it for its acceptance around the world rise above other religions is its belief that God has dealt with the human race and given instruction according to era or event. The religious philosophy that considers time, events or era gives room to the development of new rules, ideas that would be in agreement with divinity to govern the universe. With the consideration of time and its activities Christian theologians were inspired and came up with an evolved version of their holy scripture, the Old Testament and wrote the New Testament. The New Testament consists of the various accounts of the gospel of Christ as each of his disciples sees it and it also includes letters from Paul also as testimony of Christ. Basically, the Old Testament is an account of Moses revelation from God and the teaching of other prophets, the followers of God and God's own teaching during the days of olds. The Old Testament teaches about vengeance and retribution, while the New Testament teaches about forgiveness and neighborliness. For example, in the Old Testament, in the Psalm of David, David prays:

> *Hold not thy peace, o God of my praise; for the moth of the wicked and the mouth of the deceitful are opened against me: they have spoken against me with lying tongue. They compassed me about also with words of hatred; and fought against me without a cause. For my love they are my adversaries: but I gave myself unto prayer. And they have rewarded me evil for good, and hatred for my love. Set thou a wicked man over him: and let Satan stand at his right*

hand. When he shell be judged, let him be condemned: and let his prayer become sin. Let his days be few; and let another take his office. Let his children be fatherless, and his wife a widow. Let his children be continually vagabonds, and beg: let them seek their bread also out of their desolate places. Let the extortioner catch all that he hath; and let the strangers spoil his labor. Let there be none to extend mercy unto him: neither let there be any to favor his fatherless children. Let his prosperity be cut off; and in the generation following let their names be blotted out. Let the iniquity of his fathers be remembered with the Lord; and let not the sin of his mother be blotted out. Let them be before the Lord continually. That he may cut off the memory of them from the earth. Because that he remembered not to show mercy, but persecuted the poor and needy man, that he might even slay the broken in heart. As he loved cursing, so let it come unto him: as he delighted not in blessing, so let it be far from him. As he clothed himself with cursing like as with his garment, so let it come into his bowe4ls like water, and like oil into his bones. Let it be unto him as the garment which covereth him, and for a girdle wherewith he is girded continually. Let this be the reward of mine adversaries from the Lord, and of them that speak evil against my soul. But do thou for me, O God the Lord, for thy name's sake: because thy mercy is good, deliver thou me. For I am poor and needy and my heart is wounded within me. I am gone like the shadow when it declineth: I am tossed up and down as the locust. My Knees are weak through fasting; and my flesh faileth of fatness. I became also a reproach unto them: when they looked upon me they shaked their heads. Help me, O Lord my God: O save me according to thy mercy: That they may know that this is thy hand; that thou Lord, hast done it. Let them curse but bless thou: when they arise, let them be ashamed; but let thy servant rejoice. Let mine adversaries be clothed with shame, and let them cover themselves with their own confu- sion, as with a mantle. I will greatly praise the Lord with my mouth; yea, I will praise him among the multitude. For

he shall stand at the right hand of the poor, to save him from
those that condemn his soul. (Psalm 109:1-30).

David was praying for God to be merciless to his enemies and even
the generation that comes after them. This prayer exemplified retribution
and vengeance. On the other hand in the New Testament Jesus taught
about forgiveness and loving ones' enemies. According to Matthew's account of Christ, he taught his disciples about forgiveness when he prayer
for them and said:

> *Our father which art in heaven, Hallowed be thy name.*
> *Thy kingdom come. Thy will be done in earth, as it is in*
> *heaven. Give us this day our daily bread and forgive our*
> *trespasses. And lead us not into temptation, but deliver us*
> *from evil: for thine is the kingdom, and the power and, the*
> *glory, for ever. Amen. For if you forgive men their trespasses,*
> *your heavenly father will also forgive you: But if ye forgive*
> *not men their trespasses, neither will your father forgive your*
> *trespasses (Matthew 6:9-15).*

The teaching regarding forgiveness was practiced by Jesus' disciples
and people who believed in his ministries. One of the accounts of forgiveness was Stephen when he prayed for those who stone him and said "Lord
lay not this sin to their charge"(Act 7:60). Those that stoned Stephen to
death including Saul who was later converted to Christianity believed
that they were killing Stephen for God; hence, it appears like Stephen
was inspired with the Holy Spirit as he prays to God for mercy upon his
enemies. Saul or Paul conversion to Christianity might be predicated on
him witnessing a man he persecuted praying on his behalf for God to
forgive him his sin.

RELIGION AS A SOCIALIZATION AGENT

The teaching of Jesus as a Prophet regarding forgiveness and tolerance
became a cultural trait that has perpetuated to Christianity today. Unlike
vengeance and retribution in the Old Testament, the New Testament gave
several accounts of Jesus' teaching about peace. One of these accounts is
in the Book of Mark when Jesus taught about loving your neighbors as
yourself. When Jesus was asked about the greatest commandment of all,

he responded: "The foremost is, 'Hear, O Israel! The Lord our God is one Lord; and you shall love the Lord your God with all your heart, and with all your soul, and with all your mind, and with all your strength.' "The second is this, 'You shall love your neighbor as yourself.' There is no other commandment greater than these." (Mark 12:28-31). Jesus further clarified what he meant by neighbors when he set an analogy with good Samaritans and said: "A Jew going on a trip from Jerusalem to Jericho was attacked by bandits. They stripped him of his clothes and money, and beat him up and left him lying half dead beside the road. "By chance a Jewish priest came along; and when he saw the man lying there, he crossed to the other side of the road and passed him by. A Jewish Temple-assistant walked over and looked at him lying there, but then went on. "But a despised Samaritan came along, and when he saw him, he felt deep pity. Kneeling beside him the Samaritan soothed his wounds with medicine and bandaged them. Then he put the man on his donkey and walked along beside him till they came to an inn, where he nursed him through the night. The next day he handed the innkeeper two twenty-dollar bills and told him to take care of the man. 'If his bill runs higher than that,' he said, 'I'll pay the difference the next time I am here.' "Now, which of these three would you say was a neighbor to the bandits' victim?" The man replied, "The one who showed him some pity." Then Jesus said, "Yes, now go and do the same." (Luke 10:25–37). Jesus also taught about praying for enemies when he said: "There is a saying, 'Love your friends and hate your enemies.' But I say: Love your enemies! Pray for those who persecute you! In that way you will be acting as true sons of your Father in heaven. For he gives his sunlight to both the evil and the good, and sends rain on the just and on the unjust too. If you love only those who love you, what good is that? Even scoundrels do that much. If you are friendly only to your friends, how are you different from anyone else? Even the heathen do that. But you are to be perfect, even as your Father in heaven is perfect. (Matthew 5:43-48).

In our previous chapters, we tried to analyze how religions culture or any value that is practice has indelible impacts on people's behavior in the society. Moreover, there are several studies that have validated how social-ization agents such as parents, peers and teachers can influence people's behavior. The ideas in our discussion are not intended to elevate any other religion sacrosanct over the other religion or confirm any prophet holiness over the other. However, critically analyzing the teaching hallmark of each religion original or initial prophet would give us insight how people that subscribed to a religion respond to the evolving societal demand in confirmation to their religious beliefs. We have discussed several socialization agents including prophets in different religions. Jesus Christ as a Prophet whose name Christianity evolved has very salient characteristics that were crucial in orientating or socializing his followers. In Jesus' teaching besides his sagacious insights, he was firmed to instill or indoctrinate his followers with certain principles that continue to be Christianly hereditarily. From the analogies set thus far about Jesus' teaching, we have seen that he instilled the values of non-violence, tolerance, diversity, peace, rule of law, forgiveness, good neighborliness, etc. On the other hand it is important to assess, compare and contest religions principles with the pillars of democracy. Democracy requires freedom, diversity, tolerance, peace, and rule of law. Are these pillars of democracy synonymous with the teaching principles of Jesus Christ's? If there are some relationships between Christ's teaching and democracy, we might succumb that Christianity respond to democracy positively not only because it is an ideology that demand social coherence, but it is also an innate characteristic of Christian culture that its believers were indoctrinated from the beginning by Jesus, the icon of the religion; being ingrained with such value that is being passed from generation to another, it would almost be difficult for Christians to resist yielding to the golden thread or common interest of the two phenomena (democracy and Christianity).

We have earlier discussed theories that validate how environment has impacts on shaping human behaviors. It is no doubt that every individual might have some innate or genetically characteristics; however, it is also undisputable that socialization agents do channel human behaviors. The social being is accustomed to leadership model. Every group's productiveness largely depends on the leader exemplary role in the group. A leader is a role model of a group. If the leader worldviews on specific issues are skewed, he or she will create an ideological baseline that would be used as tools to inspire or brainwash the followers in an ideological cocoon that would protect the belief or worldview. The manipulative characteristic of leader does not necessary divorce inspiration. Every individual has his or her intuition about the world. These intuitions help in leadership process to model the way.

LEADERS' IMPACT ON GROUP PRODUCTIVITY

Jesus as a fulcrum of the Christian religion has intuitions: it might be considered divine or personal. There are few leaders that history has accounted them as exemplary leaders due to their leadership characteristics. The insight or judgment of a leader is crucial in predicting the group destiny. An example of poor judgment of leader to explore outside of religious ram would be President George H. Bush's judgment base on speculation that there were weapons of mass destructions in Iraq and divert America's attention on (Bin Laden) in the Afghanistan desert. The persuasion of Bush's leadership convinced the Congress to authorize him to wage war on Iraq. The thought of war was Bush's intuition; hence, uses his intelligence. However, such intuition that does not seek the perpetuation of the common good of the society does not have duration; individuals will soon become adversaries to such intuition. On the other hand, if a leader's intuition has a clear vision for the common good of the people; although, there might be some disgruntle elements of the society that might want to eliminate such leadership; however, even if the leader is eliminated, the legacy will live on. An exemplary leader should have characteristics of five basic practices: "1. Model the way; 2. Inspire a shared vision; 3. Challenge the process; 4. Enable other to act; and 5. Encourage the heart" (Kouzes & Posner, 2002: 22). The modeling the way characteristic is the aspect of leadership or in the context of this book would be socialization channel that the leader practices what he preaches – for example, if a leader should ask a group member to make coffee for the group, that leader should be willing to initiate the process of making the coffee for everyone; inspiring a share vision characteristic of a leader has to do with defining the clear purpose, short and long term goals of the group and leaving room for improvement or development thereby watching the activities of the group beyond its horizon with respect to time and space as well as indoctrinating a culture or identity of the group; challenge the process aspect of leadership welcomes and introduces new ideas in a group for group cohesiveness and at the same time making each member of the group to have the sense of belongingness or possession of the group, thus accepting new ideas in a group by a leader is a sense of conforming to time and space as the group lives on; enable others to act is a philosophy of leadership that believes in coordinated efforts through team work where the leader involves everyone in the decision making process including individuals that might be considered occupying less important positions in the group as well as empowering others to act in the absence of the leader; and encouraging the heart in this context of our discussion would be a an aspect of a leader or socialization agent that validates the group members' feelings and at the same time empathizing their concern (Kouzes & Posner. 2002). These five aspects or principles of a leader are essential in the effervescence or vibrancy of a group's vision; increment in the present and future membership, going beyond its horizon as well as gaining prominence. With the insight gained from the analogy of the five leadership principles, we have at this time understood how leaders' intuition might impact group culture and its productivity.

What was Jesus' intuition that would assume the definition and cultural trait of the Christian religion? How his exemplary leadership characteristic does continue to impact the Christian world? In juxtaposing the five leadership principles explored above with Jesus as a leader or socialization agent intuition about the world as he socialized his followers, we will digest how our social niche defines our persona. Jesus as an icon and socialization agent of the Christian faith was characterized by veracity. Justin Martyr, one of the well known recorded apologists of faith spoke of Christianity as the only philosophy which was found to have certainty and adequate clear vision as well as purpose due to its non magical or speculative or superstitious characteristics as other religions (Tillich, P. 1968).

Christianity was perceived by more philosophers as an evident based religion. Jesus' teaching was interrelated to the five principles of leadership based on the following justifiable evidence: Jesus Model the Way by practicing what he thought his disciples regarding unconditional meekness when he told his disciple Peter "put your sword into its sheath, for all who take the shell parish by the sword". "Do you think that I cannot appeal to my father, and he will at once send more than twelve legions of angels?" "How than should the scriptures be fulfilled, that it must be so?" Shall I not drink of the cup which my father has given me for the salvation of people?" (John 18:11); Jesus Inspired a Share Vision about the Christian faith when he taught his followers about the narrow way to salvation when he taught about carrying the cross and it was accounted: "and when he had called the people unto him with his disciples also, he said unto them, whosoever will come after me, let him deny himself and take up his cross and follow me" (Mark 8:34). When Jesus talked about the cross he was using a figurative metaphor that relates to suffering and endurance that would complement the religious journey. But, at the same time he challenges the process where he said to his disciples when he acknowledged that there would be persecution and said "blessed are those who are persecuted for righteousness' sake, for theirs is the kingdom of heaven; blessed are you when men revile you and persecute and utter all manner of evils against you falsely on my account, rejoice and be exceedingly glad, for your reward is great in heaven, for so men persecuted the Prophets who were before you"(Matthew 5:10-12). Jesus Enables Others to Act by teaching his disciples his values that were embedded with that of his father's values. He taught them about unconditional faith and belief that would equate his disciples to him when he taught about faith that could remove mountain (Matthew 17: 18-20); and Jesus encouraged the Heart when he discussed with his disciples that it was time for him to leave them; he talked about his betrayal by one of his disciples and subsequent death he notice that they were troubled and he encouraged their hearts and said the remedy for troubled heart is conviction, commitment and faith in his father through him (John 13: 21). Jesus transferred of knowledge or enabling other to act was observed after his crucifixion when John and Peter healed the disabled on their way to the Solomon Temple (Act 3:2-17).

The analogy with Jesus and the five principles of leadership can give us the idea of how leader's characters can impact the followers. Throughout the brief analysis of Jesus' intuition, we observed that his central idea was meekness that has extraordinary results or rewards in the celestial kingdom. Jesus passed to his followers the value and wisdom in peacemaking, tolerance, love, and forgiveness. He also empowered his disciples to pass relentlessly these values to others when he pray for them and said:

> *Father, the hour is come; glorify thy Son, that thy son also may glorify thee. As thou has given him power over all flesh, that he should give eternal life to as many as thou hast given him. And this is life eternal, that they might know thee the only true God, and Jesus Christ, whom thou hast sent. I have glorified thee on the earth: I have finished the work which thou gavest me to do. And now, O Father, glorify thou me with thine own self with the glory which I had with thee before the world was. I have manifested thy name unto the men which thou gavest me out of the world: thine they were,*

and thou gavest them me; and they have kept thy word. Now they have know that all things whatsoever thou hast given me are of thee. For I have given unto them the world which thou gavest me; and they have received them, and have known surely that I came out from thee, and they have believed that thou didst send me. I pray for them: I pray not for the world, but for them which thou hast given me; for they are thine. And all mine are thine and thine are mine; and I am glorified in them. And now I am no more in the world, but these are in the world, and I come to thee Holly Father, Keep through thine own name those whom thou hast given me that they may be one, as we are. While I was with them in the world, I kept them in thy name; those that thou gavest me I have kept, and none of them is lost, but the son of perdition; that the scripture might be fulfilled. And now come I to thee; and these things I speak in the world, that they might have my joy fulfilled in themselves. I have given them thy word; and the world hath hated them, because they are not of the world, even as I am not of the world. I Pray not that thou shouldest take them out of the world, but that thou shouldest keep them from the evil. They are not of the world, even as I am not of the world. Sanctify them through thy truth: thy word is truth. As thou hast sent me into the world, even so have I also sent them into the world. And for their sakes I sanctify myself, that they also might be sanctified through the truth. Neither pray I for these alone, but for them also which shall believe on me through their word; that they all may be one as thou, father art in me and I in thee, that they also may be one in us: that the world may believe that thou hast sent me. And the glory which thou gavest me I have given them that they may be one, even as we are one: I in them, and thou in me that they may be made perfect in one; and that the world may know that thou hast sent me and hast loved them, as thou hast love me. Father, I will that they also, whom thou hast given me, be with me where I am that they may behold my glory which thou hast given me for thou lovedst me before the foundation of the world. O righteous

Father, the world hath not known thee; but I have known thee, and these have known that thou hast sent me. And I have declared unto them thy name, and will declare it: that the love wherewith thou hast loved me may be in them, and I in them. (John 17:1-26).

THE INDELIBLE IMPACT

How does Jesus' account inspired his disciples and the religion that emerged from his teaching relates or behold democratic values? The ideas being dispensed about Jesus' teaching is intended to give insight on how socialization agents, especially social agent of faith based have impact on people's worldviews. Jesus did not teach democracy; however, his egalitarian intuition about the world went beyond democracy. Jesus grew up as a Jewish child; however, his perception about the differ from some of his orientations from the teaching of the traditional Jewish Orthodox way of life. In the Jewish tradition, women were pictured to have no significance role in the society especially when it comes to worships; women were important to be wives and procreators, they were not involved in any decision making that would affect the society (Johnson, P.1976). The emergence of Jesus' teaching in the Jewish society created a different worldview about women. Women evolved to gain significance in religion when Jesus welcomed women in his discipleship. Mary Magdalene, Mary the mother of Jesus, Salome, the mother of disciple James and John, Mary of Bathany, Martha, Susannah, and Joanna were the first set of women in the Jewish community that were involved in Jesus' discipleship. Another teaching of Jesus that continues to impact Christianity is the strengthening of the Jewish teaching or law in the Old Testament, preferably, in Exodus that says: thy shall not kill; whosoever kills shall be liable to judgment: Jesus strengthened this law and taught that anyone who gets angry with his brother shall be liable to judgment. This statement by Jesus regarding individuals that kill suggests that he dislike killing no matter what the circumstance might be. Therefore, individuals who were cultured by Jesus believe in the Christian faith and behold Jesus' teaching are more likely to abstain from any form of violence especially an act that would claim lives. Jesus also taught about dialoging with your brother to resolve dispute. With this non-violence doctrinal philosophy of Christianity, since the ascendance of Jesus to Heaven his legacy continues to be the bedrock of the Christian religion.

The legacies of Jesus' teaching that characterized social homogeneity and love for one another, have given cause to the spread of Christianity around the world. Almost every country around the world that has some symptoms of democracy is religiously dominated by the Christian faith. Why? Because, if majority of the citizen of a country embraces Jesus' philosophy of love and nonviolence that is parallel to democracy, it is almost easy for the law that governs such country to be manipulated by the belief of the majority's belief. However, it is also acknowledged that there are many countries around the world that preach democracy and do experience violence; and there are also Christians that might have involved in violence. One thing that is certain in the Christian dominated countries is that they are more likely to negotiate their differences and return to their Christian values. On the other hand, countries such as China, Saudi Arabia, Egypt, Sudan, Turkey, Burma, Greece, Ethiopia, Vietnam, Laos, North Korea, and Cuba, etc., that are dominated by other faith or beliefs continue to subdue the people by violence; and most of their victims of their violence are Christians. While it is undeniable that Christianity is the number one popular religion in the world, its meekness that is stamped as its values that was passed from Jesus Christ continues to impact believers in the Christian faith.

Christians are likely to hold democratic value because the egalitarian philosophy implemented or infused into the religion by Jesus Christ is synonymous to democracy. Most countries that are enjoying democracy today, their constitutions have one way or the other been modified to fit Christian values. For example, the United States is recognized to be the dispenser of democracy around the world because the nation was built on Christian principles; thus, it provides laws that defend and protect those Christian values.

It is sociologically appropriate for individuals to differ in beliefs, values, opinions, culture, etc. Diversity is one of the popular moving engines of socially acceptable societies. However, in order for a diversified society to maintain a manageable social environment, it should be tolerant. On the other hand, countries that are religiously homogeneous or have less population of the Christian faith have extreme beliefs about Christianity or have values that contradict Christians or other religions worldviews about God and his expectation in humankind. These mono denominational countries are likely to be absolutist and thereby accustomed to culture of oppression, violence, vengeance and authoritarianism; such society cultured its people to its values and those values are perceived normal by insider of that society, and thus consider chaotic by outsiders. Mono- denominational countries that emerged in violence and have extreme views on tolerance should not be condemned, nor should those that do not practice or preach violence and vengeance. Those that believe in violence and vengeance were indoctrinated and socialized by different socialization agents with different worldview that was consistent with time and space. We should be cognizant that human mind is like a blank sheet of paper that the society writes on. If an individual is cultured from birth in a society that writes on individual or helps to define people's character is infested with violent and culture of vengeance, it is obvious that that society will equally write those values on the people that inhabit in such social setting. Those retributive characters that the society has written on its inhabitants then become normal for that society and thereby considered as their way of life or culture. Looking at the other perspective, individuals who are exposed to a society that is characterized by culture of tolerance, forgiveness, nonviolence, and peace, will find that society writing its values on the people of that society; it then becomes normal for people to live the value that society has written on them. However, it is obvious that individuals from either side of the cultural spectrum would not agree with values from the other side of the cultural aisle.

AFRICA, A RELIGIOUS MELTING POT

Prior to the spread of Christianity, Islam, and other transnational religions in Africa, the African society was animist. Africans were accustomed to worshipping different forms of nature; some worshiped rivers, mountains, trees, valley, as wells as terrestrial creatures. The diversification of beliefs and values created a situation where every cluster of the society holds on its beliefs and worships the gods it sees fit to be beneficial. The unique personality of the African gods was that there was no universal omnipotence in one god. Every cluster of the society might worship several gods depending on their needs. Every god has power in certain areas to deliver its worshipers needs. For Example, a god that is responsible for child birth is worshipped for that purpose; another god is worship for farming purpose; the other is worship for communal good health for the community etc. (Eliade, 1967).

With the diversification of animistic worships in ancient Africa, individuals were liberty to divorce or discontinue service to certain god if that god is not powerful enough to produce the required expectation of its worshipers. If one cluster of the society believes that its god is not productive, it might choose to go to another productive god in another social cluster to worship and ask for its wants or needs. If that god produces the need requested, that god becomes the most powerful in producing that particular need. Universality in power was not the nature of African beliefs. While the Africans believe in the multiplicity of gods on a tribal level or cluster of the society as we have referred to earlier, there existed the sense of omnipotence and omnipresence of supreme power which they believe belongs to celestial insensible being. In the comfort of every tribal region in Africa the people devote to worshipping the supreme god. The people of the Mende tribe in the West Africa country of Sierra Leone referred to their supreme god or creator as Ngewo; this god is considered the beginning, the end and the creator of everything in the heavens, on earth and underworld; the Ashanti of Gold Coast, present day Ghana referred to their Supreme god as Nyame; the Ashanti relates their Supreme god to only good doings; the Congo tribes of central Africa referred to their supreme god as Akongo; also considered by these people the owner and controller of the universe; the Baganda people of Uganda referred to their supreme god as Katonda; the Kikuku of Kenya referred to their supreme god as Murungu; the people of Rhodesia, Tanganyika and upper Congo referred to their supreme god as Leza; the Ovambo of South Africa referred to their Supreme god as Kalunga; the Ibo of Nigeria referred to their supreme god as Chuku; while the Yoruba also of Nigeria referred to their supreme god as Olorun; Dan or Gio of northern Liberia refers to their supreme god as Yahweh etc.(Parrinder, 1957).

With the multiplicity of god's names across Africa, there were few characteristics that were identified to be associated with the multiple names: the creator of the universe; God of all gods, the beginner, and infinite, and protector. They all acknowledged that the supreme God was celestial sexless inexplicable invisible being that creates the universe and whose power supersedes the power of earthly gods. With the commonalities in supreme gods' characters across the African continent, it can be insinuated that monotheistic philosophy was under the surface of Africans' beliefs and worships. However; Africans also believe that after the creation of the Universe, power was delegated to wise men or their ancestors to intercede between them and the supreme god as he/she retired in his or her celestial kingdom. The intermediaries were visible beings or creatures who were believed to have vision and extra power in communicating with the supreme God. They were responsible to take worshipers requests to the Supreme for redress. A Supreme God might have several intermediaries that were responsible for several different needs for the worshipers. The god that is responsible for good health is not responsible for farming as well as crisis. For example, the Olorum of Yoruba in Nigeria might have several different intermediaries with different responsibilities such as more child birth in the community; fertility of crops; more rain and sunshine etc.

The inherited diversified social and religious fabric of the African society made the society permeable with transnational cultural and religious values. The innate libertarian religious beliefs of Africans gave rise to the continent's acceptance of other social values. While it is true that Africa is 95 percent single race dominated, it accepts diversity when it comes to religious preference. The diversified religious beliefs associated with the multiplicity of supreme and hidden monotheistic philosophy that was under the surface of African worship soon create or path way for transnational religion to find a permanent address.

There is no specific date when Christianity first landed in Africa; however, it is recorded that it was around A.D. 190. Before Christianity gained ground in Africa, it became a popular religion in the Roman Empire, which included some northern part of Africa. History recorded that St. Mark who wrote one of the gospels of Jesus was the first apostle that visited North Africa/Egypt and established a church in the Egyptian city of Alexandria; the city later became a breeding ground for the spread of the new religion (Christianity) and conduit through which it would soon become a well acceptable religion across Africa. The question we will continue to explore is how did foreign religions overflow Africa and how does religious beliefs predict individuals' responses to democracy? These questions would be answered in bits and pieces as we explored knowledge in our curiosity.

As you might be aware, it almost always is difficult for humankind to accept changes, especially when people have adopted certain values or culture that they assumed to be beneficial to them. Christianity was able to occupy the religion or belief system vacuum in Africa because: it identified with the people through their tradition; allowed them to incorporate some of their traditional beliefs in the Christian religious practices; validated their beliefs in supreme being, although, modified their thoughts of multiple supremacy in gods to up hold believe in supremacy of one celestial universal God. Both African religion and Christianity perceived common antecedence their beliefs (the ideology of supreme God); the Christian missionaries having edge in business and other trades, they were successful in rewriting or modifying most of African religious practices. The side effect of monotheistic religious practices in ancient Africa and other parts of the world is monarchal from of government or authoritarian leadership. The key idea we would like to grasp here is that in order for the religious changes that took place in Africa to be successful, the Christian missionaries submerged themselves in the African culture, learned their languages; trade with them western values; hence, modified behaviors such as human sacrifice and other cannibalistic behaviors that were common religious practices among Africans (Friedenthal & Kavanaugh, 2007). In traditional African religion or beliefs the people personify God as moon, Sun, the life giving spirit; the power that animated the fire; the creator of the universe and at the same time believe that there exist evil spirits that are controlled by devil, With this cultural belief, Africa did not cede entirely to other religions especially Christianity and Islam. Such African beliefs and practices are common among African Churches as the concept of supreme god; sickness is a product of misfortune and belief in the power of ritual prayers most of African churches and Islam places of worship continue to embrace the African values.

Why Christianity did seeped or modified other cultures around the world? Did Christianity succeeded in reforming cultures because it is a true religion? Is Christianity better than other religions? Our interest in this diagnostic discourse is not to give any statistical ranking, be it nominal; ordinal; ratio; or interval ratio value to any religion. The concern of our discourse is to provide explanation for why and how individuals or different religion respond differently to democracy. One answer that might be set as foundation for our argument as we explore other explanations for individuals respond to democracy is that, everyone behaves in accordance to the merit of his or her immediate environment or society. Religion in Africa is a matter of culture, tradition, heritage or possession. Every ancient African belongs to a religion and they believe in supremacy of god. Every tribal supreme god chooses certain family to intercede between the rest of the tribal people and the supreme god. It is from this sub-god's family, leaders would always emerge because it is mystically considered as the chosen family of god. If the individual that is in position serving as sub-god dies, his son or immediate family member will take the post as the next chosen person. God communicates directly with this chosen person and he or she takes the message to the rest of the tribal people. It is through the sub-god leadership is chosen.

Although Christianity and Islam are said to be dominant religions in Africa; the religious transformation process that took place in Africa allowed Africans to incorporate some of their Africanism into the newly-introduced Christianity and Islam; those African traditions of ownership, belongingness or possessive ideology still champion African leaders' decision making and their response to democracy. Moreover, Islam and Christianity being the major transformation phenomenon in Africa, there are regions or certain geographic localities that are dominated by either of the religion; hence, an Islamic dominated region or countries will produce Islamic leadership that would characterize Islamic culture, values, tradition and beliefs. On the other hand, an African geographic localities that are populated by Christianity are more likely to produce Christian leadership that would promote Christian values, culture traditions and beliefs; those who exclusively hold on to the original African religion and profess it in public places continue to be the minorities, but are considered significant figures with divine power who often serve as secret sages to the leaders, thus facilitate their political decision making. In such a society where infusion of multiple philosophical beliefs and ideas are cultures, there would constantly be dissonance that would preempt social and political instability because beliefs vs. views would be difficult to have a negotiated balance where common interest would be identified.

What would happen to such society with a multiplicity of values and dissonance of ideas? In a state of mind where there exists dissonance of ideas, decision making becomes dependent on some powerful intervening phenomenon that would create a state of harmony in thought process.

The heritage and the sense of ownership religious culture of Africa gave rise to a situation where, if an African migrates from one cultural setting to another in the same continent, he or she will almost experience different religious pattern that would make his assimilation into that culture slower. Hence, the birth of Christianity in Africa that introduces the sense of universality in religious principles serves as antidote to the state of dissonance and taught them the idea of harmony in religion. When the Christian missionaries introduced the sense of religious harmony it was embraced by Africa and the new introduced religion gained some level of religious hegemony in the continent.

While Africa embraced Christianity and its values as well as the religion allowing Africans to mix some of their traditions with that of Christianity, there was one key belief or value of the African that was not synonymous with Christian doctrine: the "one man, one wife" Christian value. This was the point of divergence between the visiting religion and the host religion. However, with this difference, Christianity continued to spread in Africa until the Islam invaders invaded Egypt in 639. They continue to invade and conquered most of the North African religion. They established Muslim states and begun to convert the established Jews and Christians into Muslims; however, the Christian and Jews that upheld their religion were laved special tax in the emerging Islamic states to practice their religion (Friedenthal & Kavanaugh, 2007). Those who converted to the invading religion were free from the so-called religion practice tax. The tax laved against the non converts created a profound hardship on the African Jews and Christians and as the result most of them converted due to the economic, social and political hardship. One important aspect of the second transformation period or the introduction of the new religion (Islam) was that Islam had several values that were common to African traditions that were being expelled by Christians and Jews. The introduction of Islam gave rebirth to some of the expelled traditions of the Africans. Islam values such as one man multiple wives was cultural belief of the African that could not be abandoned in the wake of accepting new religious values. The cultural or religious similarities African perceived in Islam, the northern part of Africa soon become Islam dominated. Islam conquering northern Africa drove Christianity to Central, South, East and West Africa. The region in Africa that is dominated by Christianity, subscribes to Christian values, principles and by-and-large have some form of Christian states.

On the other hand, the African region that is dominated by Islam has Islamic states, values, principles and at the same time has Islamic dominated governments and keeps the status quo such as polygamy practices; slavery, and the believe of owning a religion. These values were the common golden threads that were used by Islam invaders to easily convert Africans to Islam. The idea of ownership or authoritarianism began to seep gradually in government. In order for the leaders that held power in Northern Africa not to relinquish power, they declared all the countries they held a kingdom; therefore would be ruled by one family. This monarchial philosophy of governance derived from traditional African religion and Islamic beliefs. For example, as we have discussed earlier, an individual that is considered the interceder between God and the community in African tradition or religion is automatically the leader of the community or is more likely to choose the community leaders; when the leader dies he or she is often succeeded by an immediate family member. If the interceder is not the leader, he or she is often the sage to the leader. This tradition is common in Islam: the Imam or leader of various Islamic prayer centers or mosques are considered individuals that descended from Muhammad or are people of extra ordinary faith (Murata and Chittick, 1994).

With the unconditional believe the Muslims have in their Imam, an Imam is never changed, and the position is passed down from family member to another. Both African tradition or religion and Islam having these common religious heritage characteristics and culture of leadership, if an individual from any of these groups assumed power, it becomes almost impossible to relinquish power to another person. For example, Algerian President Abdelaziz Bouteflika assumed power in 1999 and still maintains the position; Libyan President Moammar Quaddafi assumed power in 1969 through coup d'état and still maintains the position; Egyptian President Hosni Mubarak assumed power in 1981 and still maintains the position; Western Sahara President Mohamed Abdelaziz assumed leadership in 1976 and still maintains the position; Sudanese President Omar Hasan al-Bashir assumed power in 1993 and still maintains the position; Nigerian President Amadu Toumani Toure came to power in 1999 and still maintains the position, etc. Monarchial or authoritarian leadership is common in Africa or Islamic world because it evolved from their culture and religion. Such belief is considered normal and a way of life. Leaders of most Islamic dominated countries including Africa are almost always selected instead of be democratically elected by the people they govern and they are more likely to remain in power for life or removed by violent insurgence or military coup d'état.

These examples do not otherwise suggest that Christian-dominated countries in Africa do not have similar problems; however, countries that are dominated by Christianity, such as Nigeria, Ghana, Malawi, Liberia, Central African Republic, Cameroon, Togo, Uganda, Kenya, Ivory Coast, Sierra Leon, etc., have some form of fragile democratic process of selecting their leaders and have fundamental history of democratic electoral process. The main idea we are trying to dispense here is that religions impact individuals' behaviors and responses to democracy. The democracy in Christian dominated countries in Africa is fragile because it is a compound that is made up of two different religions/religious elements with disagreeable values: traditional African religion and Christianity that is more or like considered to be manipulated by western culture. On the other hand, the monarchial or authoritarian leadership in Northern African and the Arab world is a product of Islamic culture and tradition.

There are several school of thought or beliefs out there that if depth into would create a state of dissonance in an individual regarding his faith. For example, in Michael Martin's book, he came out strongly against Christians' beliefs based on knowledge and reason; he tried to refute Christians' belief in the imminent coming of Jesus; the doctrine that there are three persons in one God: the father, the son, and the holy ghost; the belief that Virgin Mary give birth to baby Jesus; and claim that Jesus was a son of God (Martin, 1991). There is no attempt in our discussion to give supremacy to any religion; however, to eliminate intellectual conundrum that would create a mental block that might impede our ability to understanding our focal point, we would like to give insight to our reader the possibility of multiple persons being in an individual. The possibility of multiple persons being embedded in an individual is exemplified in the roles an individual play everyday in the society. For example, a father can be a child when he is with his parents; a husband can be an employee when he leaves his home and goes to work; a driver can become a passenger when he or she is not behind the wheel; a police man can be consider a civilian when he is not uniformed; a student can be a teacher etc. An individual having multiple personality is obvious in our society today. In the field of mental health, an individual can be diagnosed with multiple personality (Morrison, 1995). From these analogies above, it can be suggested that it is possible for three persons to be in one person, as is claimed about Jesus.

However, the peculiar idea that needs to sentiment in our thoughts is how religious practices, beliefs and orientation are contagious and crucial in defining the persona of individuals; thus reflect in their responses to their worldviews about democracy. In the worse case scenario we might consider every claim Christianity has about Jesus, a fact or fallacy regarding him being a son of God; what can we say objectively about his teaching of societal harmony that is validated by every religion? Is there any reason why we should believe that Jesus perception about people and the world were comparable to what an empathetic God would do? There are facts regarding the Christian religion that equates it in the discourse of democracy: the moral philosophy, focusing on one's own affairs; teaching of monogamous life and sexual purity; special concerns toward brothers; composure and the ability to console in time of distress; nonviolence confrontations; doing unto to others as they wish would be done to them; valuing their lives as they value other's life etc. (Meeks, 1986). Democracy is defined as the free will of the people; in the Christian faith individuals are independent of their own continence to decide on what they want to be. In other words, the faith is not hereditary to pass from generation to another. It is not an inheritance; it is a matter of choice. The missionaries who evangelized the Christian gospels do not coerce people to accept Christ or they do not ostracize individuals who were not willing to accept Christ. The missionaries use different forms of peaceful Christian diplomatic persuasion to win people to Christ. However, there are histories that recorded Christian's involvement in some sets of disputes; these disputes have no evidence that they were orchestrated by Christians because individuals refused to accept the religion. Christians have been persecuted and continue to be persecuted around the world in places we indicated earlier in this chapter; yet, because of their faith philosophical doctrine inspired by the transmittable worldview of Jesus, they continue to be kind and use diplomacy instead of retribution to resolve dispute.

THE IMPORTANCE OF CHANGE

It would be a big vacuum in our discussion about Christian nations and their behaviors without mentioning the antique counter productive practices of Christian nations such as Europe and the Americas relative to their involvement in human servitude. While democracy is taking its course in the Americas and Europe, these two nations were involved in transporting human from Africa as tools to work on their plantations. Both Indians and the Africans were considered subhuman until some priest no longer could understand slavery in the same paragraph with the gospel of Jesus Christ. The idea of slavery in Christian nations came to a sporadic examination when Antonio de Montesinos, a Dominican preached a sermon to some Spanish Christian congregation and accused them of violating the principle of the gospel of Jesus Christ because they made slave of men and women who have done nothing to undergo such afflictions; and show no interest in their future or welfare; Montesinos accused these Christian nations in his preaching by asking: "are they not human beings?"; "have they not reasonable souls?"; are you not bound to love them as yourself?" (Chadwick, 1995:189). After the Montesinos' sermon, another Christian slave importer, Las Casas has sailed from Europe to Columbia; his mind was interrupted by Montesinos perching and set his slaves free; after this redemption sermon, Pope Paul III issued the Bull Sblimis Deus in 1537 that acknowledged that people on earth are human by their nature; as a people they have the right to their freedom and their property and must not be robbed or made slaves; and they are all able to receive the faith and are to be persuaded in it (Chadwick, 1995). This repentance or reversion of slavery laws did not take immediate effect; however, it was the beginning of the end of barbaric society and at the same time the emergence of the rebirth of Christian values inspired by Jesus Christ.

The United States that was established on Christian values has a horrible historical record of violence and segregation against African Americans and other immigrants. During the period of the 1850s and World War I, there were negative immigrant perceptions all over America. The Europeans who resided in America before World War I were considered Americans and those who came between 1880 and 1914 were considered immigrants and underwent all forms of discrimination, such as: being considered stupid, dirty, violent, sexually uninhibited; passing of legislation in1887 that required literacy test to immigrant to determine their knowledge of English before entering America; doubling the head tax on immigrants; the Quota Act of 1921 that was introduced to limit the influx of immigrants to the United States; mob action and lynching of African Americans increased between 1890 and 1901; injustices of the court system against African Americans – thus ignoring the rights of African Americans as citizens by judges and other law enforcement system that brought about in 1896 the Supreme Court ruling in the case Plessy V. Ferguson that mandated "separate but equal" – and therefore segregationist – treatment; discriminatory legislation such as the Jim Crow laws were enforced to deny African Americans access to public education; the unfair discharged of 167 African American soldiers stationed near Brownsville, Texas, in 1906 and other discrimination based on race, ethnicity, and national origin were considered legal and became commonplace in America (Iglehart.& Becerra, 2000).

Social and economic discrimination were the order of the day in early America; however, based on the foundation of the country that values Christian principles embedded the legacy of Jesus' teaching, America has evolved from a nation of segregation to a society of integration; from the nation of intolerance to embracing the culture of tolerance; from the nation of violence to a nation of peace; from the nation of slavery to the nation of freedom; from the status quo of maintaining uniform culture to embracing diversity. The reformation of American culture undoubtedly is predicated on the nation's creed that was established on October 11, 1892, that is based on Christian values: "I pledge allegiance to the Flag of the United States of America, and to the Republic for which it stands: one nation under God, indivisible, with liberty and justice for all. Prior to this current version of this creed, it had its initial versions that were revived on June 14, 1923, June 14, 1924, and this final version of 1954, respectively."

Chapter 5
Democracy in the Eye of Buddhism

THE EMERGENCE OF BUDDHISM

Throughout our discussions in previous chapters we have been analyzing religious doctrines under microscope in order to make clear to our conscience the microscopic ideology in every religion that are said to shape human's behaviors, and thus channeled their responses to democracy. In this chapter we will magnify Buddhism as a religion as well as it doctrines. We will also outlook the characteristics of the founder and how his philosophy or legacy had had indelible impacts on Buddhists behaviors and response to the society.

Buddhism like any other deity or religion has its doctrines and behavioral patterns that distinct it from other faith. It is widely believed that Buddhism derived from Hinduism or it is a replica of the Hindus religion. However, myth or fact, as history has recorded; the religion emerged from a teaching and curiosity of a royalist name Siddhartha Guatama who live around the sixth century B.C. Other historical accounts suggested that Guatama lived around 560-480 B.C.E. The word Buddhism derived from Buddha which means "the Enlightened One." Buddhism derived when young Guatama, a royalty who has every wants of his life to his disposal went to play his favorite game Archery outside the palace. During his game play outside the palace he saw what life looks like outside royalty. He saw for the first time suffering people, aging people, sick and dead people and a Hindu who had neglected the worldly Endeavour and starved themselves to nothing but skin and bones (Ions, V.1986). When Guatama saw such a difficult life outside the palace, he was astonished and deeply troubled and he decided to leave the palace to go out and explore the reality of life. When he left the palace in search for the meaning of life, he was first inspired by five Hindu priests who accepted that the way to learn the truth of life is to stave the body. Guatama exercised the starved Hindu method until he was fleshless; hence, this exercise did not teach him any wisdom of life or solve his internal puzzles. He then retracted and recommended normal eating. In continuation of his inquiry for the true meaning to life, Guatama decided not to starve or and not to be too rich; he adjusted himself to the midpoint of richness and starving. He ate enough so that his attention wouldn't be distracted by hunger. He located a very quiet place under a sacred tree called Bodhi tree. He sat under the tree for 49 days meditating. During the course of the 49 days, he vision armies of Mara (evil force or spirit) of the world. The Mara armies attacked Guatama with all sort of weapons including rain, rock, storms and they later offer him wealth for him to abandon his curiosity. Guatama overcame the temptation and the evil spirits fled. At the end of the forty nine days Guatama gained the true insight of life and he was recognized as the Buddha or the "enlightened one". Thereafter, people who believe in the act of such free thinking were referred to as Buddhist and the act or belief was considered Buddhism.

FUNDAMENTALS OF BUDDHISM

Out of curiosity, one might ask about the kind of enlightenment the Buddhists are interested. One might also be interested to know the focal philosophy of Buddhism. The Buddhists are interested in what they referred to as the holy truth; and thereby sought the meaning of the holy truth (birth, aging, sickness and death). In the search of enlightenment of the holy true, the religion believes that the path to enlightenment is eightfold or has eight different religious obstacles that every individual has to overcome to be a true awakened, enlightened one or Buddha. In order for one to be a true Buddha, he or she has to have: 1. Right belief (freedom from chimera); 2. Right intention (evil thinking is not associated with Buddhism); 3. Right conduct, peaceful and pure; 4. Right living, causing no injury to any creature; 5. Right effort toward self control (Yogic Meditation); 6. Right thinking, applying the mind to religious experience and right meditation on all the mysteries of life; 7. Right means of livelihood; and 8. Right talk (Reat, 1994 and Erricker,.1995). This eightfold path is the fundamental values or pillars of Buddhism.

Buddhism, like Hinduism, has some common beliefs and philosophical conjunctions such as the circle of birth or reincarnation. The Buddhists also believe in the rotation of life, death and rebirth as well as manifestation of living creatures to another. As in Hinduism, the Buddhists accept the idea of Karma, which teaches that good conducts or bad behaviors are rewarded afterlife. However, there is a philosophy that distinguishes both religions (Buddhism and Hinduism). Unlike Hinduism that believes in Cast system or confined social strata of life, Buddhism believes that all humans are equal in every divine possibilities and thus avoids Hinduism conjure ritual philosophy. The Buddhists believe that an individual position or success in life is highly dependent on the individual's efforts and not proponent upon social class or any form of stratification he or she was born. This thread line that distinguishes these two religions is very salient in vindicating the Buddhists' religious pillars that are highlighted in the path to enlightenment. The reiteration of the eight paths: right to understanding or Samma ditthi; right intention or Samma sankappa; right speech or Sammavaca; right action or Samma kammanta; right livelihood or Samma ajiva; right effort or Samma vayama; right mindfulness or Samma sati and right concentration or Samma Samadhi to enlightenment pave a role for Buddhists behaviors to be in coherence or come closer to principles of democracy. The Buddha believes that when an individual accomplishes the eight paths, the possibility of moving up on a social ladder is inevitable. The philosophical difference that set Buddhism apart for Hinduism brought the Buddhist even closer to conceiving democratic values.

What is important for us to extract from the fundamentals of Buddhism and transfuse into our political thoughts is that the religion does not first advocate the interest of a particular group; it first obligates every individual to place him or herself under the behavioral microscope; it does not project or envisage obligatory universal hegemony of the religion; it is exploratory, thereby providing freedom to everyone to use his or her faculty to enhance their desires; and it focuses on developing individuals mind for communal living. The envisaged product of individuals efforts to enhance the eightfold path to enlightenment can be summed up to one of the major pillars of democracy which is tolerance; hence, crucial in building a cohesive society. For example, putting each of the Buddhist eight paths under ideological microscope, we might interpret or correlate them to democratic values such as diversity, tolerance and freedom.

In a broader sense, the Buddhist eightfold paths attempt to bring to our conscience the importance of wisdom, scruples behavioral patterns and psychological disciplines which are all transitive in the actualization of better human relationship. The first pillar of Buddhism which emphasizes right understanding could be interrelated to individuals' ability to be objective and prudent in gaining insight in other people's values and perspectives or worldviews. When individuals have right understandings about themselves and others, they are more likely to understand the characteristics of humankind and thereby remain open minded with right intentions in dealing with any form of diversity. The Buddha philosophy or ideological principle on which the religion is built that emphasizes individualistic efforts to realize the eightfold path to enlightenment can lead to a collective goal of enhancing societal harmony.

ETHICS OF BUDDHIST

Every religion has distinguished characteristics or axioms that are passing from generation to another. As time evolves these axioms might be modified to be consistent with the emerging social orders or demands; however, there are peculiarities in every religion that remained unchanged and thus defined that religion. For example, in Christianity there might be several religious rituals that might be eliminated or transformed due to persecution of Christians around the world, but what appear to remain unchanged is the belief in one God, loving their neighbor as themselves, being their brothers keepers, and forgiveness. In spite of all the obstacles Christianity may have encountered, the religion holds onto these core values to continuously identify the faith of distain character. In the same regard, Buddhism has core distinguishing characteristics that also continue to define the religion. The principle of the religion that is based on self purification stands it among other religions. In Buddhism, self purification is the foundation on which better society can be built. The role to self purification is connected to the eightfold path to enlightenment. As we have discussed earlier, the Buddhist use the eightfold path to indoctrinate new converts. The path to enlightenment that is introduced to every convert is broken into five major commitments that are not only an obligation to the Buddhists, but a means to the ends. Being a Buddhist is to agree not to: 1. engage in killing human beings no matter what the case may be; 2. avoid embezzlement of any kind; 3. disengage in sexual misconduct; 4. disengage in use of any form of intoxicant, for it might lead an individual in an inappropriate behaviors that might not be in the path of self purification or it might lead to temporary cognitive dysfunction that might distort one's focus from the path to enlightenment; and 5. disengage in any kind of mendacity (Lopez Jr., 2001). These doctrinal vows are made across Buddhist's world especially in countries that subscribe to the two major division of Buddhism (first and second councils or Mahayana Buddhism and Nikaya Buddhism). These five religious commitments or vows when withheld and practiced by individual Buddhist not only enlighten the individual, but their consequence is a collective good for the society. The Buddhist believes that self-purification can lead to good for the many, benevolence, and pardoning that comes out of compassion. These morals that are crucial part of the religion are direct results of the eight pillars.

What is the culture or tradition of Buddhism that mold the Buddhists for their behaviors or practices to be in the same paragraph with democracy? As we continue to highlight the eightfold path of enlightenment, it is cogent that the path coalesced to enhance human rights that are crucial in democratic society. The practice of Buddha ideology of exploring enlightenment is an effort geared towards creating bonhomie social structure. Democracy and Buddhism might have different nomenclature, but they appeared to dispense the same idea of tolerance, nonviolence, and respect for one another in all walks of life and love for animals and other organic creatures.

DEMOCRACY, HUMAN RIGHTS, AND BUDDHISM IN SOUTHEASTERN ASIA

The eightfold path to enlightenment and the four spiritual truths of Buddhist ontology are encomium principles in discussing democracy in Buddhist dominated countries or even in places around the world. However, it would be intellectually dishonest if we did not mention countries like Thailand, Burma, Sri Lanka, and other Southeastern Asian countries that appear to be dominated by Buddhist populations but continue to experience gross human rights violations. It also would be important to bring Buddhist ideology about life or ontological perception under the microscope to explore a diaphanous insight in Buddhist culture and resolve its contributions to ill democratic values in those regions.

Thailand is a Buddhist country, which means its culture, traditions, or values are dominated by Buddhist ideology, which proclaims that enlightenment, comes through individuals' ability to detach from the world; a philosophy that has reduced a majority of the country's population to mendicant and created a culture of pauperism. The Buddhist definition of detaching from the world was illuminated in Guatama curiosity to search for enlightenment by means of depriving himself of riches and royalty, going with hunger for several days and latter placing himself on unstable diet. The idea of restraining the body with self-deprivation as well as distasting worldly endeavor appears to be the invisible hands behind the slow democratic process in Thailand, Sri Lanka, Burma, and other parts of Asia that are Buddhist-like religiously dominated.

It is evident to say that the absolutist political culture that existed in Thailand paused in 1932 when a military government took over and formulated constitution as a baby step to democracy. It is about sixty-eight years since Thailand initiated the constitutional democracy; it is ironic that a country that is dominated by religious monks with spiritual wisdom has experienced violent military coups and continues to be ruled by military.

In spite of the several changes in political environment through military eruptions, that social structure of the country that is characterized by pauperism did not evolve for the better. The undemocratic transition of political process in Thailand that is cultured around a military takeover also has contributed two dimensions of social structure in the country: those who participate in government and dominates agribusinesses reside in urban areas and those who abstain from government activities, largely monks and their families as well as other people, dwell in rural communities. In such a hierarchical society where there is no idea of gentrification of ideas, culture and the community, it is difficult for individuals to climb the social ladder and become self-sufficient.

It is more than two thousand years since Guatama gave birth to Buddhism and its religious principles. The world is revolving around technology and new ideas. Cultures of other places are being transported and exported by means of technologies such as television, radio, cell phones, video games, dress codes, and other transnational values. This means that new social environments are being created and introduced and individuals have the ability to affect their environment as well as their environment has the capacity to affect them, thereby social and culture change or modification becomes inevitable (Longers, 1990). The Buddhist principles or eightfold path to enlightenment addressed democratic values such as human rights and the well-being of the people; however, a society that is acclimatized to established cultural values, when it is transfused with liberal ideals, that society is subject to experience social dissonance. On all social levels and institution such as school, family, religion etc, the byproduct of such environmental evolution is behavioral transformation, cultural modification, and local value detachment or psychological reformation.

Due to the exportation of transnational values in Buddhist-dominated countries like Thailand, young people, men and women, especially young women are being transformed or remade by imported cultures that are appealing to them. In order to transcend the cultural, social and economic austerity, young girls of Thailand are detaching their religious values and becoming sexually promiscuous, thereby being exploited by sex exploration or sex mania. Despite the stages of political revolutions that have created two segments of Thai society, coupled with the ongoing human rights problems relative to sexual exploitation, the political, social, and economic progress in the global market continue to be incremental. Buddhism continues to be one of the promising transformational elements in Thailand's Buddhist communities, such as Thamkaechan, Kastra, and Phra Prachak's Khamkhian, which are Buddhist enclaves that are engaged in several self-help projects to keep their heads up from the wave of cultural and religious value degradation practices such as sexual misconduct that are emanating from the culture of poverty.

Sri Lanka is another country that is popular with the Buddhist culture. In fact, Sri Lanka is considered the first country in the region outside India that adopted Buddhist culture and the tradition of Buddhist teaching regarding faith, morality, meditation, and wisdom that ultimately are inscribed in the eightfold path and renounce the dominant social order in the country (Parrinder, 1984). The establishment of the Buddhist religion can be traced as far as the third century BCE when monk Mahinda and other Buddhist priests from India explored the island. The introduction of Buddhism in the island allegedly converted Davanampiy Tissa, the king, and he later became an exponent of the religion; his conversion and subsequent support for the religion remain crucial in Buddhist history.

In order to understand the almost implacable civil disturbances in Sri Lanka, it is important to underscore some historical events in the society and explore the underlying pedigrees that are ravishing the island and from religious moral opulence to an impecunious and violence human degraded society. Before the emancipation of Sri Lanka in 1948, it experienced its share of European colonial domination. The Portuguese controlled the island from 1505 through 1815, when they were vanquished by the British. We might not be able to streamline the chronology of events on the island; however, since the independence of the country in 1948, democracy in the country continues to remain fragile, especially the ethnic conflict of July 1983 that has escalated to a violent civil war that continues to claim thousands of innocent lives.

However, during earlier May, 2009, the government of Sri Lanka through its military spokesman announced the military troops triumph over the Tamil rebels; the government announced that the Tamils' rebel leader Velupillai Prabhakaran was escaping in an ambulance and was killed by governments troops. Most Tamils denied the government's claim regarding the death of Prabhakaran; the story was later confirmed by the Associated Press.

The death of the Tamils' rebel leader has been claimed by Sri Lanka government as the end of the civil crisis; however, in the absence of legislative policies that would address the concerns of the Tamils that they have fought for over the years, it would be difficult for the Tamils to accept the death of Prabhakaran as the end of their struggle.

What could be the underlying factor of the 1983 ethnic conflict? After the British granted independence to the island, political power landed in the hands of Sinhalese tribe and the Colombo Elites that were all educated in Britain. Since the transition of power from British rule to the local elites and the Sinhalese, the pattern of leadership continues to be skewed in an ethnic direction, thus favoring the Sinhalese and the Colombo privileged minority, and thereby marginalizing the Tamil minority tribal group. The attempts by successive political regimes to ostracize the Tamil minority and at the same time the advocacy and plead for rights by the Tamils that continues to fall on the duck-back of the political leadership of the Island resulted in a creation of a jingoistic ideology of the Tamil to form an extreme political arm movement called Liberation Tigers of Tamil Eelam (LTTE) that would protect the interest of the minority as well as protest the Sinhalese dominated central government.

There is no doubt that the fundamentals of Buddhism disapprove an act of violence, and any form of behavior that would endanger anyone's happiness. However, the protracted conflict in Sri Lanka is the result of policies that were enacted under the leadership of S.W.R.D Bandaranaike in 1956, which was intended to improve the life of Sinhalese over other tribal group in the country. The economy and language policy introduced by President Bandaranaike came under strong protest by the Tamils in Colombo. The protest toke place in Colombo, Trincomalee and Jaffina, and resulted in Sinhalese mobs killing nearly 150 Tamils; on August 19, 1956, a fourfold demand was made by the Tamils to secure peace: (1) a federal constitution be established to protect both Tamils and Sinhalese; (2) both tribes – Sinhalese and Tamils – should be considered equal; (3) citizenship should be granted to the Tamils with Indian origin; and (4) the domination of Sinhalese rule in Tamils majority area should be abolished (Peebles, 2006). These demands were not addressed by the central government and the Sinhalese continue their domination in Tamil-speaking areas. The refusal of the central government to formulate an agenda that addressed the concerns of the Tamils created unhappy feelings among Muslims Tamils against the Sinhalese Buddhist dominated government.

While the violence in Sri Lanka has numerous chronicles of events, it is obvious that since the independence of the island, its constitution has undergone sixteen different revisions that include the thirteenth amendments of 1978 that attempt to create a Buddhist state and marginalize the Tamil tribe, which comprises a significant percentage of the island's population; hence, the Muslims and the Christian minorities; at the same time creating a legal provision that refused to acknowledge the plantation Tamils as citizen of the country stands amongst the numerous factors that are ravishing the island's people and their civilization (Peebles, 2006). The violence on the island is reported to have claimed more than sixty-five thousand lives and to have displaced more than one million from home to neighboring countries, according to International Committee of Red Cross report (ICRC). Accordingly, Sri Lanka is dominated by the Sinhalese that subscribe to Buddhism; the Tamils subscribe to Hinduism and a small percentage of each tribal group consists of Islam and Christianity. This demography implies that since the Sinhalese are dominant in population, in government, and subscribe to Buddhist religious ideology, the government of the island is dominated by Buddhists. This analogy is a common sense in Algebra that states: if "A = B and B = C, then C also = A. At this juncture, it would be a philosophical mistake not to acknowledge hidden florid contribution to the civil unrest on the island. With the dominance of Buddhists in the Sri Lankan government and the constitution of the country being amended with provisions that support and protect the Buddhist interest and thus marginalize ethnic and religious minorities, we would like to bring the Buddhist eightfold path under the ideological microscope to explore insights whether the Buddhist's principles are just a theory that supposed Buddhist tradition and not in practice in Sri Lanka or that the perception of the island's Buddhists is a divergence of the original Buddhist principles of enlightenment.

In this chapter, we are devoting time to look at three Southeastern Asia countries that are dominated by Buddhism: Thailand, Sri Lanka, and Burma. We are exploring to understand how religious beliefs and practices impact both social and political wellbeing of a society. On a theoretical standpoint, Buddhism teaches about ethic of restraint in bicameral: restraining the factors that inhibit compassion and the second the need to cultivate the habits that are appealing to enhancing human happiness such as love, patience, tolerance, forgiveness, humility and other values that promote harmony among people; ethic of virtue that emphasizes that every individual reframe from negative thoughts and emotions and cultivate and reinforce ones adorable qualities and that ethic of compassion that emphasizes empathy or our commitment to bring home to oneself another person's feelings (His Holiness The Dalai Lama, 1999).In the Dalai Lama teaching of ethic that is based on the eightfold path to enlightenment he warmed those who claimed that his teaching about unconditional love is improbable, he urge them to experiment and they will discover that when the mind reaches beyond the confines of self interest, it becomes filled with strength; thereby peace and joy become the irresistible companion of oneself (His Holiness The Dalai Lama, 1999). In theory, what could be learned from the teaching of the Dalai Lama is that religious self efficacy can lead to collective efforts in the realization of social harmony.

However, with the Dalai Lama inspirational teaching that is based on Buddhist religious principle, it is expected that countries that are dominated by Buddhism, the values claimed by His Holiness would be the order of that society. On the contrary, Sri Lanka whose population consists of over ten million Buddhist Monks that make up about 65% of the country's population continues to experience untold suffering due to political ideologies that appear to marginalize the Tamil minorities (Powell, 1989). Due to the disenfranchisement of the Tamil tribal group, the LTTE continues to disrupt the political, economic, and social climate of the country as the violence has claimed lives on both sides, the Sinhalese

Buddhist dominated government and the Tamil LTTE fighting group; thou, the LTTE fighting group of the Tamil has been condemned by international communities and being considered terrorist group. While the Sri Lanka society was characterized by sporadic violence or some form of civil uncertainty among tribal and religious groups, the current escalated violence could be the result of unresolved political and economic differences between Sinhalese and the Colombo elites on one hand and the Tamil and other minority tribal groups on the other hand -following their independence in 1948 and thus, outburst of violence in July, 1983 with the LTTE militant ambush of the national government military troops that killed thirteen Sinhalese soldiers, an act that brought about Sinhalese outrage in Tamil communities and claimed lives and destroyed thousands of Tamils properties (Wickramasinghe, 2006).

As we have been scanning the violence of Sri Lanka, a country dominated by one of the world's peaceful religions, Buddhism, we should be cognizant that the violence has a multiplicity of causes: the Tamils claim that the country government is dominated by the Sinhalese, who are mostly Buddhist; the Thirteenth amendment of the constitution in 1978 that created a sense of superiority of the Buddhist religion in the country; the continuation of the discriminatory Cast social system; the quota education system that disenchanted desire Tamils students from entering the urban region universities; the proliferation of different Tamil ethnic orientated insurgence groups such as the Tamil United Liberation Front (TULF), LTTE, Tamil Eelam Liberation Organization (TELO), the People's Liberation Organization of Tamil Eelam (PLOTE), the Eelam People Revolutionary Liberation Front (EPRLF), the Eelam Revolutionary Organization of Students (EROS), and an estimated over 320,000 Tamils who have sought refuge around the world with its majority refugee population in Canada that have created a web of coordinated communication system called Computer Mediated Communication (CMC) and the imagination of the Tamils to create a Muslim state or community, remain crucial in understanding the dynamics of the conflict on the island (Wickramasinghe, 2006, and Peebles, 2006).

Dumoulin and Maraldo provided a modified version of the Buddhist eightfold path with ten explanation and maintained that there are five heinous crimes: (1) matricide, (2) patricide, (3) the murder of an Arhat, (4) the wounding of a Buddha, and (5) a creation of a schism in the order (sangha), and ten immoral actions: (1) killing, (2) unchastely, (3) stealing, (4) lying, (5) slandering, (6) harsh language, (7) frivolous talk, (8) covetousness, (9) ill will, and (10) false views (Dumoulin, and Maraldo, 1976). With these Buddhist religious principles in mind, the Sinhalese Buddhist dominated government's attempts to create a Buddhist nation and at the same time refusing to address the minority Tamils' demands, among other things, contributed immensely to the civil unrest on the island and a complete divergence to Buddhist spiritual values, practices and beliefs.

It is unrealistic to say that the conflict in Sri Lanka has no religious implications. Our intellectual microscope has reveled that there are three major pedigrees with multiple ideological and philosophical cells that gave birth to the nightmare on the island. The microscope discovered that prior to independence, land or territorial struggles, women, and caste system were factors in the society that created discriminatory behavior on the people that society described or identified to belong to the lower caste or lower social stratum. As Marguerite Robinson was quoted by Wickramasinghe regarding a village dispute between member of the upper caste and member of the so-called lower caste: "on August 31, 1921, got instance, it was reported that one such person, U.G. Punchirala (member of the lower caste) complained to the headman that a buffalo belonging to Heena Appuhami (member of the upper caste) had damaged his paddy field; the headman investigated and the lower caste man brought the buffalo to the field to prove by comparison of Hoff prints that the upper caste man's buffalo has done the damage; the headman ruled in favor of the upper caste man and said that it was not the cause of the owner of the buffalo that the lower caste man paddy field was damage" (Robinson, M.S. in Wickramasinghe, N. 2006: 112). This and much other ethnic and religious violence were part of the colonial era. Another example that links religion to the present conflict in Sri Lanka is unequal seating policy in colonial Sir Lanka schools; children of the lower caste were required to sit on the floor while children of the so-called higher caste usually from elite tribal group were seated in chairs. This form of discrimination came under strong criticizing by the youth congress and resulted to them supporting the "equal seating" policy. They advocated that school children should be given equal seating opportunity regardless of their social status or stratum. The colonial government in 1930 formulated policies that held grants for schools that would engage in differential treatment among students. However, the equal seating policy had both antagonists and pro-tagonists: those who maintained that there was natural and philosophical different such as race, religion, language, custom, civilization, diet and hygiene between Jaffna Tamils and Sinhalese detested the equal seating policy and those who advocated for the enforcement of the policy for the interest of all school children.

Besides the tribal or ethnic disputes between the Sinhalese and the Tamils, there were occasional disputes between the Buddhists and the Christians (catholic) minority. One of the several disputes was at the verge of the nineteen century when violence erupted between the two groups for what they referred to as sacred space. Each religion attempts to protect its religious territorial limit by barricading its confined area from trespassing; however, the Christian's sacred space were often trespassed by Buddhist parade as well as Buddhists defining it illegal for Christians to build churches on where they considered Buddhist dominated region. As you can see the possessive sentiment and rigorous religious ideology that one religion, Buddhism or Hinduism or Christianity or Islam has territorial rights more than the other begun to surface in the conflict and became one of the divisive tools that continues to underline the conflict on the Island.

Several discriminatory policies such as the J.R. Jayewardene 1943 resolution to make Sinhala the official language for Sri Lanka, the citizenship Act of 1948 that was followed by the Indian and Pakistanis citizenship Act of 1949, and Parliamentary Elections Act of 1949 were discriminatory and considered anti- Indian policies of the state council because their provisions gave popular representation to the Sinhalese and thus viewed by the Tamils as legislations that attempt to disenfranchise them. These policies created radical sentiment among some Tamils that were in the government and decided to brake away. One of the Tamils who broke away was S.J.V. Chelvanayakan, who established a radical group called Ilangi Tamil Arasu Katchi or ITAK. The ethnocentric and territorial struggle sentiment and other disputes that took place during colonial domination in Sri Lanka were not resolved up to independence. The act of retribution continues after independence in 1948 with policy makers reforming constitution to benefit their specific ethnic and religious group. For example, chapter II of the Sri Lanka constitution exclusively provides provision for the full protection of a specific religion (Buddhism) with clause or phrase that appeared to give subsidiary protection, not full, for other minority religions. Chapter two of the Sri Lanka constitution read as follows: "The Republic of Sri Lanka shall give to Buddhism the foremost place and accordingly it shall be the duty of the State to protect and foster the Buddha *Sasana*, while assuring to all religions the rights granted by Articles 10 and 14(1)(e)". The removal of the protection of civil rights and human right clause in the colonial or Soulbury constitution also underpinned extremist ideologies among breakaway politicians; local Tamil plantation workers, and Tamil youngsters who see their future under the Sinhalese Buddhist dominated regime bleak. The reformation of the colonial constitution legalized the nationalization of private lands that resulted to government seizing over one million acres of land from local framers; restrictions placed on media institutions that were viewed by central government radical or critical on reporting so-called government secret; as well as restriction on Tamil Youth to use foreign currency to study abroad, disallowed the importation of South Indian Tamils films, books and magazines were among triggering factors that surfaced the Tamils youth terrorist ideology that attempted a car bomb assassination on Somaweera Chandrasiri, a Sinhalese Buddhist government official that was visiting Jaffna, a Tamil Hindu Dominated city in 1971(Wickramasinghe, 2006, and Levy, 2004). Thus, the car bomb did not get its target; however, it was the birth of terrorism in the region.

As we continue to move our diagnostic microscope slowly, but steadily with attentiveness across the Sri Lanka conflict, we will continue to capture the egotistic, ethnocentric, and religious centric ideologies that divide the people of the Island. For example, the Sinhalese Buddhist and the Colombo elites control the central government; the Tamil Hindu-Tamil Plantation workers want to control their won territory and have their own government as the result of repressive constitutional provisions; the Christians and the Muslims are in the minority, thus stuck up in the middle of the conflict and often victimized by Tamil terrorist or Tigers of Eelam. We will also find that the Sri Lanka conflict is becoming breeding ground for international conflict as well as seed for controversial politics where feudalism and anarchic system of control are being rebirth and gained prominence; countries like India-a Hindu dominated country; Pakistan- a Muslim dominated country; China, Burma, Thailand with popular Buddhist communities appear to be seeping invincible invisible hands in the conflict to protect individual religious group that identifies with them (Levy,.2004, and Nye, 2003). The more the conflict in Sri Lanka continues, the more transnational hands find individual interest in the parties involved in the conflict and support their interest.

The discussion in this section is not intended by any means to endorse any party; Sinhalese Buddhist dominated government on one hand and the Tamil LTTE on the other hand. It is an open true that both parties involved in the conflict have engaged in gruesome inhumanity; however, our focal thought is to bring out the unspeakable microscopic unresolved pedigree that continues to outbreak conflict, even if attempts are made by international communities to bring the hostilities to a manageable state. Until the combustible religious, ethnic, social stratification by caste system and territorial factor underpinning the conflict become visibly discussed and addressed, peace in Sri Lanka would be like a pail of cow feces that is place under the sun and its surface appears dried, but the inner membrane or layers remain wet. It is undeniable that the LTTE are being labeled terrorist by international communities in their struggle for territorial possession, liberty, and subsequent independence from main land Sri Lanka; we should also note that constitutional provision that gave Buddhism dominated by Sinhalese superiority over other religions and ethnic minorities in the country disenfranchises the minorities and thereby becomes a trigger for continue outburst of civil unrest that continues to claim innocent lives including women and children.

BURMA AND THE EMERGENCE
OF BUDDHIST POWER

Before British occupation in Burma, it was a kingdom that was governed by kings and its people were in a dictatorial political environment. Sooner than later a Scottish South African explorer like Archibald Colquhoun has traveled across the globe and understood that British colonial domination and success in commerce in Asia was being obstructed by despotic king of Burma and suggested in one of his writings that "all that stood in the way of the revival of British commerce and industry; all that kept the working people of Birmingham and Leeds from better future was the despotic king of Burma; remove the king and Burma would become British's best friend; and from Burma the riches of China and that meant British commerce and industry would be there for asking"(Myint-U, 2006:8). Colquhoun's suggestion in his writing to conquer Burma for the sole purpose of British commerce was appealing to Randolph Churchill; Burma's rich forests, huge oil deposit, and the unsustainable natural deposits of ruby soon interested Churchill and created a situation that would bring down Burma's King Thibaw. The entire Southeastern Asian region was dominated by colonial powers, such as the Prussian Empire, Britain in India, and France developing an interest in Burma. Britain could not invade Burma immediately due to France's assumed interest, despite Britain's explosive commercial interest in Burma that developed from Colquhoun's writing. A political agenda was reached between France and Britain and Britain waged war on King Thibaw; it conquered the country and occupied it from 1824 through 1948. However, this occupation was interrupted briefly by the Japanese when they drove the British out in 1941 and subsequently gave a fragile independence to Burma in 1943 (Bunge, 1983, and Myint-U, 2006). The independence Burma gained from the Japanese was not sustainable, British continued it occupation in Burma until January 4, 1948, when the British finally declared Burma an independent nation.

Before Burma's independence, the people of the country underwent different political and social environmental transition. They encountered several wars with the British. Few of the popular wars were the first Anglo-Burmese war that resulted in British annexing Burma; the second Anglo-Burmese war in 1852 and the third Anglo-Burmese war in 1885.

What would these ill political transitions means to the people of Burma? Besides the exploitation of Burmese resources by the British and other colonial powers, the one hundred and twenty-four years of occupation was characterized by disagreement between the indigenous and the colonies, thus created societal turmoil that subjected the Burmese to unbearable suffering that promoted religious hitter, and social class system that subsequently gave birth to the culture of poverty in the Burmese society. The byproducts of the one hundred and twenty-four years of colonial authoritative rules in Burma are religious intolerance, perceived religious superiority, ethnocentrism, and retributions. These byproducts are divisive elements that discourage the political, social and economy wellbeing of any nation.

Burma's independence in 1948 came through the successive hands of revolutionaries like Mahatma Gandhi and Pandict Nehru, who headed the Indian National Congress. There were several statespersons after Gandhi and Nehru who went through the struggle to give birth to independent Burma. Local Burmese politicians like Yadana Yimun, Aung Gyi, Aung San Suu Kyi, U Nu, and other young student leaders including Dr. Ba Maw emerged later in the twentieth century as leaders of the Freedom Bloc that demanded Burma's independence from the British colonial power. Some of the youths who were in the vanguard of Burmese liberation paid for the freedom with their lives when demonstrations were initiated to protest British domination in the country. The military was ordered to disrupt the protesters; under the command of General Reginald Dyer, they fired 1,650 live rounds among the weaponless protesters, killing hundreds of them in April 1919. This and other colonial leaders' aggressions against the Burmese were obvious.

Burma is another country in Southeastern Asia that continues to have its share of civil violence in the region and also is dominated by Buddhism. In order to get a clear picture of the culture and politics in Burma, it is important to look closer at the of type sect within Buddhism that is practice in the country. On the overall, Buddhism has three major sects: the Theravada, the Mahayana, and the Vajrayana. Burma, like all other countries in Southeastern Asia, believes or practice a branch of Buddhism called Theravada. The Theravada Buddhists believe in one historical figure, Shakyamuni or Guatama, and their doctrine and teaching are associated with the four noble truth and the eightfold path to enlightenment; the Theravada tried to fused every culture with the tradition of the Buddha-the teaching of moral of life and the monastic way of life; the Theravada tradition is an evolving phenomena that embraces urban culture and village life; on the village level it teaches about primitive beliefs in ancestry and the belief in sprit and at the same time taught the local dwellers about agricultural life, the life cycle of an individual and the "maintaining of personal and communal wellbeing"; whereas on the regional and royal level, the Theravada Buddhist is concern with Brahmin learning and court rituals and thus above all it identifies a particular national culture as with the Sinhalese in Sri Lanka (Dumoulin and Maraldo, 1976:44).

Up to this point, with the insight we have gained in the Buddhist eightfold path to enlightenment, it is evident that the religion's doctrine has rich values that would have the possibility of building a moral and cohesive society. However, our microscope was able to capture facts about

Buddhism that appeared controversial and might be the breeding ground for violence in Buddhist dominated countries, especially the countries that practice Theravada Buddhism, like Thailand, Sri Lanka, Burma, Cambodia, Laos etc. The ideological microscope captured the concept of creating a national religion and separation of the pattern of religious rituals between locals and regional Buddhist to be a major stimulant for the civil unrest, thereby have the proclivity of creating a social class system where individuals mobility from one class to another might be scarce. For example, in the Theravada Buddhist countries, the local or villagers who are Buddhist are orientated with religious doctrines that philosophically confined them to agricultural rituals and their individual wellbeing; and on the regional level, the Buddhist are religiously orientated with belief of urban civilization such as engaging in noble profession like being a lawyer, doctor, politician etc, as well as holding the believe that in order for Buddhism to survive it has to be nationalized (Dumoulin and Maraldo, 1976). With these philosophies, especially creating a centralized religion as fundamentals of Buddhism and Burma being dominated by the religion, it emerged from independence with chaotic religious agenda that would result to the persecution of members of minority religions and group that did not sympathize with Buddhist ideologies and philosophies.

The idea to centralize one religion and give it superiority over other religions or groups in a country has become expensive for Burma and continues to purchase its consequences at an incremental high price. Today Burma is considered as religiously diversified and ethnic sensitive country. Before theorizing the philosophy of diversity, Burma has adapted Buddhism as a national religion. For example in the eleventh century Buddhism was established as a national religion by King Anawrahta, with no regard for other ethnic and religious minority groups. Establishing Buddhism as a national religion means that the government has created a social, economic and political hierarchy where ethnic group such as Bamar, Rakhine, Shan, Mon, and the Chinese who are Buddhist would be up on the social, political, and economic ladder; where other ethnic groups such as Kachin, Chin, Kayin, and Eurasians, who are Christians; and the Sunni, Indians, Indo-Burmese, Persians, Arabs, Panthays, Rohingyas, and the Chinese Hui, who identify with Islam will be on the lower stratum of the government's social, political, economic and of course religious stratification, thereby, predicting a possibility of differential by the government. The idea of adopting Buddhism as a national religion continues from the eleventh century through independence in 1947. In 1983 the idea of Buddhism as a national religion was modified by the introduction of Burma Socialist Program Party that recognized Buddhism and socialism as the core value of the government and people of Burma. Prior to the modification of considering Buddhism as a national religion in 1983, in 1982 the Burmese government enacted a divisive legislation that was specifically designed to deny Indians, Chinese and other minorities citizenship.

Buddhism's ideologies and philosophies were given superiority by the government; thereby, other ethnic and religious minorities being considered inferior became evident with government legislative actions that continuously deny Burmese Muslins and the Christian minority citizenship. The creation of a national religion and alienation of ethnic and religious minorities came under strong resentment with sporadic establishment of anti government groups that emerged from ethnic and religious minority groups individually. Consequently, right after independence in 1947, the communist organized an arm dissident group to unseat the government; subsequently, the Karan ethnic minority have also established their own group to seek territorial independence and protect the integrity of that minority group, a group that eventually gained prominence and controlled lower Burma and other parts of the country (Bunge, 1983). The establishment of Buddhism as a national religion was revived by U Nu and the philosophy continued through his twenty-one years of leadership from 1962 through 1983. With one religion being identified as the national religion, governmental religious bias was unavoidable.

Since Burmese independence, Buddhism has been considered national religion and its members continues to be privileged and receive opportunities from central government as other ethnic and religious minorities continues to receive extra judicial treatments such as persecution of Christians and Muslims ; a behavior that has exiled most of the Muslim minority in Bangladesh and at the same time the ethic and religious persecution has been a uniting factor for ethnic and religious minorities against the central government whom they all considered their common enemy (Mawdsley, 2001).

As we already know the adorable doctrine of Buddhism, and Buddhism being the popular religion in Burma, outsiders who do not have the historical sense about the country might have different perceptions. An outsider who does not have insight in Burma history might conclude that Burma is a country of mutual respect with emphasis on diversity and has a social system that is ethnic sensitive and religiously tolerant. However, this is not the case; Burma has a history of hostilities against non Buddhist ethnic and religious groups. What went wrong with Burma Buddhists practice of the Buddha's peaceful philosophy? Has the religion been used by Burmese politicians as means to accomplish their individual political agendas? Theravada or Hinayana Buddhism that is being practiced in Burma is considered the original Buddhism practiced by the founder Guatama. If the Burmese have been practical in the Theravada Buddhism as they professed, the country would be a nation of people of right views, right resolve, right speech, right conduct, right livelihood, right mindfulness, and right concentration as Guatama had taught. The Buddha taught that a true Buddhist should have no attachment to worldly materials or interest; he was enlightened that the stronger attachment or interest an individual develops in worldly activities, the weaker or difficult it becomes to be religiously enlightened and satisfied; the Buddha also teaches that the more individuals attach themselves to worldly interest or satisfaction, the more they become unreasonable (Bunge, 1983, and The Dalai Lama, 2001). This philosophical doctrine means that Buddhist should avoid worldly activities such as participation in politics and seeking higher political offices. However, Theravada Buddhism acknowledges the value of career, pleasure, society, and above all, individuals' wellbeing. We have not been able to find the disconnection between being career oriented and distaste of worldly interest. What the Buddhists do with their career after it being developed without interest in worldly activities is an inquiry the needs further explanation in Buddhism. However, the Theravada Buddhists believe that when individuals are attach to worldly interest, it is not a sin, it is being human and they will detach to worldly activities as they grow older.

With the noble teaching of the Buddhist religion and the current human degradation that is prevalence in Burma (Myanmar), what could be the possible underlining factor? Is it because this Buddhist dominated country is yet detached to worldly activities; or their interest in worldly activities has had this Buddhist dominated country irrational? These are questions we intend not to answer, hence leave it with our readers to debate on them internally. However, there are logical speculative variables that could predict Burma civil unrest and religious intolerance. The fundamental belief in worldly detachment was threatened by British domination that exploited Burma vast natural resources that literally created the culture of poverty among the citizenry; British favoritism in Christianity over Buddhism during colonial remained crucial in defining the cause of Burma's behaviors towards other religion in the country. On the other hand, Buddhist/Burma army massacred of eight Christian civilians in Karen villages in 1984 could be another reason that Christian and other ethnic and religious minority have united against the government to show their resentment in any form necessary. Religious intolerance in Myanmar (Burma) cannot be explained without identifying the sole root of the violence. The international community continues to describe anti government military group activities in Burma as terrorism and equally describes the government inability to dispense justices as human rights violation. There is not disconnection between these two forces. Maybe, they both have abstract of their activities in the region that has distinctions; one is a self imposed government that assumes to have totalitarian rule and the other is a group that opposed totalitarian administration that is dominated by individuals of one religious sect. Government preference in one religion had made several foot prints or imprints on other minority religious groups. Buddhist anti Muslim sentiment continues to fuel the trouble in Burma as well as government creating a political defense by backing the Buddhist majority when they violate individuals of other religions rights. Buddhist anti Muslim violence in Burma has been pronounced in Arakan State, Prome, Taungoo, as well as Rangoon, the capital of the country where the government is seated.

As we mentioned from the beginning of our discussion, we have tried to make an imprint on our readers' mind that individuals of different geographic location, culture or religion respond to democracy in the context of their individual environmental orientations. Individuals' diverse responses to democracy are result of their immediate environment. While environment creates imprint on individuals, individuals also affect the environment. Environmental factors that that are determinant for human behavior are their religion, culture, social stratification relative to education attainment, economic opportunity or deprivation of other basic social needs. According to the Critical Theory of human behavior, human behavior in a given society is a result of social structure that is caused by "inequitable social structure" that is determined by economic organization of the society; hierarchy in cultural organization whose byproduct is exploitative economic structure (Longres, 1990:14). Critical Theory also maintains that when individuals are subjected to inequitable and exploitative economic structure and social injustices, the victim is not only interested in condemning the perpetrators or the abusive environment, but they resolve to a strategy of here and now which requires a major revolution that would change the hierarchical glass ceiling social environment.

The Critical Theory discussed above identifies with the situation in Burma (Myanmar). Burmese history has been characterized by transitions of administrations that created culture of social hierarchy that systematically attempts to keep the lower stratum of the hierarchy in its position while the upper or higher stratum maintains its position and dominates. For example, the Pagan Dynasty, (1044–1287), the Taungoo Dynasty (1484–1752), the Konbaung Dynasty, and the Anglo-Burmese war were historical periods characterized by aristocratic regimes. This form of political environment means that the people were subjected to totalitarian form of leadership. After the fall of the aristocratic political regimes in Burma, the colonial power took over and perpetuated exploitative economic, social and political environment.

After more than three centuries of authoritative leadership, authoritarianism eventually became an acceptable culture of the Burma people until new culture or form of leadership begun to emerge. The introduction of human rights, religious tolerance, freedom of speech, freedom of association, freedom of free and fair election and liberalness that are crucial elements of democracy were viewed alien by Burmese politicians (Suu Kyi, 1991). The democratic philosophy that professes liberalness and opportunities for individuals to pursue their individual life desires was considered western idea and thereby came under strong resentment by government authorities. Those who accepted the democratic philosophy are from the other side of the social spectrum or lower hierarchy who had been subjected to differential treatment by people in the higher hierarchy. Because of the long ill political, social, economic, and religious environment that created division between the people and their government, the introduction of democracy was an eye opener that gave rise to the here-

and-now method of resolving conflict through quest for automatic change or violent revolution. The theory of here-and-now method has been used in Burma since its independence in 1948; there has been no smooth transition of power, all its leaderships had been succeeded by military copes; it has had repressive authoritarian regimes since 1962; the 1974 socialist constitution was suspended by the military government and since 1988 constitutional protection for freedom of individuals and their religious rights has not existed.

It is indisputable that Buddhism's teachings or values are noble, moral, and thus heed to humanity; however, Burma being dominated by Buddhism and the country's leaderships continuously being characterized by totalitarian and repressive governments prompts the outside world to explore theoretical evidence that would highlight or give food for thought to the fundamentals of Burmese divide. To answer our curiosity, we might want to discuss another Buddhist sect, the Mahayana, which dominates in parts of Asia in countries that appear to pronounce some symptoms of sanity. Insight in the Mahayana sect as we explored Theravada sect in our previous section might give us an idea of different Buddhist sects and their impacts on the countries these beliefs are considered crucial in leading the people. We mentioned earlier that the Theravada Buddhism that is practice in Burma acknowledges one historical figure who is Shakyamuni or Guatama. To an extent, the Mahayana adopts the belief of multiple Buddha and bodhisattvas. So, in this light, what could be pinpointed as the difference between the Theravada and the Mahayana Buddhist sects? The difference between these two sects is that Mahayana believes that despite Guatama, the original Buddha giving birth to Buddhism, there is a possibility that individuals who sincerely follow the principles of the deity can attain enlightenment and become worthy of nirvana as they continue to be part of the human society and continue the value of helping people to be liberated from suffering as well as being spiritually successful. The one historical Buddha doctrine of the Theravada on one hand and the multiplicity or dynamic philosophy of the possibility of another Buddha emerging among believers in the Mahayana sect has political significance in the countries where these individual sects are popular.

The fundamentals of Buddhism that subscribe to the four noble true of life: that suffering is worldwide phenomenon; suffering is cause by craving or egotistic desire; the cure to suffering is to rid oneself of craving and egotistic ideology and the path of getting rid of craving or egotistic desire is to follow the eightfold path of enlightenment ;and the eightfold path of enlightenment that teaches: right knowledge; right intention; right speech; right conduct; right means of livelihood; right effort; right mindfulness; and right concentration remain consistent in every Buddhist sect. However, the multiple philosophical doctrine of Mahayana Buddhism could be interpreted as ideas that accepts diversity, and the concept of diversity is parallel with tolerance; nonviolence, respect for individuals; new ideas; development, meaningful and rational modification of old ideas that would help the society to respond to present history of better human endeavors. For example, from the onset of Buddhism its monks and believers were literally mendicants; however, Mahayana Buddhism dominated countries like Japan and China have made rational modifications to the archaic philosophies of the religion and the people of these countries are emerging from sustained austerity to technological opulence that is making there people enjoying their share of globalization.

On the other hand, the concept of dogmatism that is being observed in Theravada Buddhist dominated countries can be interpreted as a breeding ground for totalitarianism, intolerance, violence, and societal divisiveness as these ills social characteristics are evident in Theravada countries like Thailand, Sri Lanka, and Burma (Myanmar). There is no doubt that writers who have insights in religions have admitted that the Theravada Buddhism has evolved over the years and has eliminated or modified "archaic values such as the prohibition of any contact with money, of speaking or traveling with woman, or taking meals after noon, or killing any living being and so forth"; the elimination of the original Buddhist doctrine that prohibits killing any living being is crucial in predicting the roots of violence in Thailand, Sri Lanka and Burma (Myanmar) that are all Theravada Buddhist dominated countries (Dumoulin and Maraldo,.1976:37). If the assertion that the modification or elimination of the original Buddha teaching that prohibits taking away or killing any being were observed by Thailand, Sri Lanka, and Burma the possibility of these countries sustaining violence and adapting culture of human degradation, is not certain, what would better explain the culture of intolerance and violence in these countries that are one religion dominated? The evidence being provided that reflected the two major sects in Buddhism does not suggest one being superior to the other; it is intended to show how religious practices and beliefs impart social, economic and political fabric of any society.

The sole essence of Buddhism that was passed down to the believers by Guatama, the original Buddha was for Buddhism to serve as a conduit through which individuals suffering would be minimized or eliminated. Buddhism like Hinduism attached value to life and thereby considers taking away life as demerit to the religion's laws or ethics; however, the assassination of Mr. Bandaranaike, the president of Sri Lanka in 1959 by two Buddhist monks was a turning point in Buddhist ethical history that contradicts the religion eightfold path to enlightenment. The reason for the monks' action was not officially established; however, before and during Bandaranaike's leadership in Sri Lanka, the Buddhists advocated for them to have national superior rights over minority religions like Christianity and Islam as well as majority Sinhalese rights over the Tamil minority. The Buddhists had their share of the Bandaranaike's administration; apparently, the Buddhist agenda of creating a Buddhist state was not pushed too fast to achieve its overall goal, and thereby resulted in Buddhist extremism. The concept of seeking religious rights over other religions being embraced in recent years by Buddhist monks contradicts Guatama; the Buddha's teaching that is emphasized in the eightfold path to enlightenment. Ignoring the fundamentals of the religion by individual sects within Buddhism has created line of demarcation between Buddhists and the path to enlightenment, hence, has brought suffering such as terrorism and other forms of social disturbance to nations that professed Buddhism, yet, their behaviors contradict the eightfold path that is the fundamental of the religion.

FAMOUS QUOTES IN BUDDHISM

The few quotes mentioned are proverbs emphasized by famous Buddhist sages that helped to channel Buddha's teaching and preserved the culture of Buddhism.

THE WAY OF THE LAW

All that we are is the result of what we have thought: it is founded on our thoughts... If a man speaks or acts with an evil thought, pain follows him... Hatred does not cease by hatred at any time; hatred ceases by love…Carpenters fashion wood; wise people fashion themselves. (From the Dhammapada in Luce.et al., 1968:37)

One's own self conquered is better than all other people conquered; not even a god…could change into defeat the victory of a man who has vanquished himself…Let no man think lightly of evil, saying in his heart, it will not come nigh unto me. Even by the falling of water drops a water pot is fill; the fool becomes full of evil, even if he gather it little by little…he who holds back rising anger, I call a real driver; other people are but holding the reins…The scent of flowers does not travel against the wind, but the odor of good people travels even against the wind; a good man pervades every place. (From the Dhammapada in Luce et al., 1968:40)

BUDDHA'S TEACHING

Returning Good for Evil

A foolish man, learning that the Buddha observed the principle of great love which commends the return of good for evil, came and abused him. The Buddha was silent, pitying his folly. When the man had finished his abuse, the Buddha asked him, saying, "Son, if a man declined to accept a present made to him, to whom would it belong?" And answered, "in that case it would belong to the man who offered it."

"My son," said the Buddha, "I decline to accept thy abuse, and request thee to keep it thyself. Will it not be a source of misery to thee?…A wicked man who reproaches a virtuous one is like one who looks up and spits at heaven; the spit soils not the heaven, but comes back and defiles his own person."

...The abuser went away ashamed, but he came again and took refuge in the Buddha.(From the Sutra of Forty-two Sections, in Luce et al., 1968:41)

Drought and Rainfall, A Parable of Buddha

Brothers, there are these three persons found existing in the world. What three? The one who is like a drought, the one who rains locally, and the one who pours down everywhere: and how, brothers, is a person like a drought? Herein, brothers, a certain person is ...no giver of food and drink, clothing ...bed, lodging and lights to ...the wretched and needy beggars. And how, brothers, is a person like a local rainfall? In this case a person is a giver to some, but to others he gives not...And how, brothers, does a person rain down everywhere? In this case a certain person gives to all... So these are the three sorts of people found existing in the world. (From Itivittuka, in Luce et al., 1968:55)

CHAPTER 6
PRESCRIPTION/DISCUSSION

Throughout our exploration in this book, we have discussed cultural and religious orientations and how they affect human behaviors and their responses to democracy. Culture being theoretically identified as one of the major determinant factors for human behaviors cannot be erased from our intellectual table. However, our exploration suggests that socialization agent such as religion surpasses culture when it comes to modeling people's behaviors and response to democracy. Religion has become stronger in modeling people's behaviors because individuals become part of a religion on the average as a matter of choice, especially in the west where democracy is emerging as a new religion gives people the ultimate rights to use their faculty and make choices in the context of their individual rights. It is not disputed that religion cannot sometimes become automatic as culture, but it is almost impossible to change your birth culture as you might be able to change your religion or religious views as you become an adult.

We also have discussed with theoretical evidence that people behaviors are the direct product of their immediate environment such as their individual socialization agents that include but not limited to parents, peers, teachers, school, religion and religious leaders, coaches, immediate relatives, persons being admired, culture, etc. These environmental forces help to define individuals' personality. People differ not only in the personality they possess, but also differ in their unique prototypical thoughts, feelings, values, behaviors, and motives. These factors that shape human kind are collection of behaviors from the multiple socialization agents that sometimes transmuted individuals' original orientations and transfused different values. Therefore, since there is no one universalized socialization agent that would create unison in people's behavior; as well as these multiple orientation agents teach people with different values from geography to another and in effort to enhance democracy, it is important to create a philosophical evolvable system that would help to modify societal behavioral patterns that are considered by majority unacceptable.

Religion as one of the socialization agents has some entrenched belief principles or values the need to respond to social evolution for the security and better living of all peoples. For example, as we mentioned in our chapter on Christianity, Moses law taught the Jews retribution such as "eye for an eye" in their holy Torah. This passage of the Old Testament Bible or the Torah evolved or was modified by Jesus Christ in the New Testament:

> *For if you forgive men their trespasses, your heavenly father will also forgive you: But if ye forgive not men their trespasses, neither will your father forgive your trespasses (Matthew 6:9-15).*

This value has been held by Christians since Jesus modified the retributive teaching of Prophet Moses. The adherence to Jesus' teaching is a vindication of one of the theories discussed in this book that states: individuals behave certain ways when they conceive that the product of their behaviors or actions will have more benefit than the negative consequence. In Christianity, forgiveness is one of the major pathways to God the father in heaven. Therefore, in order for individuals that subscribe to Christianity to inherit God's kingdom they should behold Jesus' teachings; for the benefit of forgiveness in Christians' view is more than retribution.

We mentioned in the chapter that discussed Islam that the changes or modification that has taken place in Christianity is yet to occur in Islam; therefore, Muslims still subscribe to the archaic vengeance and retributive philosophies of Prophet Mohammed. The spiritual teaching of vengeance is being used by Muslim extremists and individuals with egotistic ideology to validate their terrorist activities and push their personal agendas. There is no doubt that Muhammad was a prophet of God that inspired the Arabia region in which he lived at the time with his prophetic teaching; however, one major idea that Islam is yet to accept is that the instructions that were given to Muhammad were intended to vanquish the idolaters of Mecca or Quraysh that protested the spread of Islam at that time. There is nowhere in the holy Qu`ran that God spoke directly to any of the prophets that came after Mohammed to perpetuate retribution and vengeance in the religion. However, it is important to understand that every negative jihad in the Holy Qu`ran against Jews and non Muslims or people of other religion are not instruction from Allah; they are all man-made Fatwa or Islamic creed that are intended to create ideological and religious supremacy. For example, Qu`ran chapter 9:5 reads: "but when the forbidden months are past, then fight and slay the pagans wherever ye find them, and seize them, beleaguer them, and lie in wait for them in every stratagem of war; but if they repent and accept Islam and establish regular prayers and practices regular charity than open the way for them; God is oft forgiving, most merciful". (Holy Qu`ran). If you scan through this passage, there is no indication that God was the one giving instruction to slay his creations. This passage projected that man in his own idea is giving instruction to gain supremacy.

Osama bin Laden and his terrorist sleeper cells occasionally have used the negative aspects of Jihad to destroy the world on grounds that America instructed the creation of Israel; America attacked the Islamic religion in Somalia; America supported Russia aggression against Muslims in Chechnya; American support for India alleges tyranny in Kashmir; America supports Israeli aggression in Lebanon; America exploits Muslim land wealth (oil) in Muslim countries; America creates military bases in Muslim countries; America protects the interests of Israel; America exterminates Muslims in Iraq, etc (Williams, 2004).

Individuals wrote several passages in the Qu`ran stating that God instructed all Muslims to fight for him (God) and he will reward them with unimaginable wealth; the conception that fighting and dying for Allah is worthy and those who do will receive the most prestigious heavenly glory is a psychological supernatural utopian ideology that that has been championed by men through religious creed to satisfy their ego. If the Jihadic philosophy of dying for Allah's sake is right and has unimaginable benefit, it would be very crucial for us to put it to test in this manner: since every individual believes in self actualization and self gratification, let suggest that Osama bin Laden decorates himself with the best nuclear weapon and explode himself wherever he thinks he can find Americans, died for God sake and receive the proclaimed extraterrestrial glory or reward. Do you think he will do it? No! I don't think so. He wouldn't do it because it is a supernatural utopia or philosophical unicorn that does not exist. Everyone wants to go to heaven and enjoy the heavenly glory; but who wants to go now? If fighting and dying for Allah to get outstanding reward is true, why when a terrorist is killed, the terrorist group gets angry and revenge and don't celebrate for the great long awaited reward?

As we have analyzed all the five major religions' culture and their doctrines or orientation principles under our intellectual microscope, it now is assured that we have got to know that religion as a socialization agent has a serious impact on individuals' behaviors. In order to effectively combat the current raise of terrorism and other future terrorist activities we must:

1. Disengage from using war as a primary means to combat terrorism; this should be the last resort. The tendency of fighting terrorism with heavy weapon is in it self creating a breeding ground for perpetuating terrorism to the future. Even, if we assume that we have power and means to exterminate the terrorist or Islamic militant, is it possible to kill the entire terrorist generation? This will be a non-realistic endeavor. The Nazi tried to exterminate the Jewish from the face of the earth; it was impossible, there were thousands of Jews that left. Even those that were killed some of their children lived or might currently be alive. The history is there and the memory continuous. If we continue to use military force to fight terrorist or kill those whom we assume to be terrorist, we will be creating hatred history for their children, and the history will be passed to their children's children and the philosophy of vengeance will continue to bear fruit and the history will continue to hunt us.

2. Instead of investing billions of dollars in Islamic government abroad, the torchbearers of democracy need to reinvent Adolf Hitler's signature policy regarding investing in youth. Hitler maintained that "he who owns the youth gains the future." Hitler successfully controlled Nazi Germany not only because he was monstrous or cruel, but because he invested in German youth from the age of eight thought their adulthood and eventually enlisted them in the Nazi army to execute his orders. Hitler institutionalized a group called youth for Hitler; the youth were trained or infused with his ideology, and when they grew up as an adult, they accepted the Hitler's values instilled in them as normal and every order from him was executed without remorse. Hitler created a socialization institution where agents were available

to indoctrinate or infuse the youth with Hitler's world views. This philosophy that was use negatively by Hitler could be inverted and use positively by democracy torchbearers. The torchbearers should create policies that would give Muslim youth international scholarships that would allow them to leave their immediate terrorist environment; be trained abroad for sever years with democratic values. After these new values are instilled into them, it will create an ideological dissonance and their old violence culture or ideas would be over shadowed or transmuted by the new democratic ideas; when they returned to their various countries, those values being instilled will be transmitted into their societies and thereby adapted as culture.

3. Invest in the same youth, train them to conceive reformist philosophies to rewrite or modify the violence aspects of Jihad in the holy Qu`ran so the Qu`ran will respond to contemporary civilization. Until this recommendation is systematized and institutionalized to modify the violence portion of the holy Qu`ran, even if the governments in those nations that subscribe to Islamic Jihad are changed and new government takes over, it would be like teaching old dogs new tricks, as well as putting new wine in an old bottle and expecting a different taste. For example; you have complained that a government or regime of certain countries are governing on constitutional provisions that violate individuals' inherent rights; you conducted election or overthrew the government with military insurgence; the government has been changed; new set of people are in office, but the constitution that the previous government based its leadership on and it was popularly condemned or criticized is still in place, adapted by the new government. Have you affect any change? What would you expect from the new government that would base its governing on the fundamentals of the old constitution that embraces violation of individuals' rights? The law of Physics says that in order to have a work done you have to do two things: 1. apply force on an object;

2. move the object and cover a distance (Force X Distance = Work). If you apply force to an object without moving it to cover a distance, you have not worked. In this case setting a new government is the force that was applied; using the old constitution without amending the provisions that violate basic human rights is as well as applying force without moving the object in a distance, no work has been done. Therefore, in order to rationalize the current efforts being applied to vanquish terrorism, it has to take multi dimensions that would include campaign for the modification of certain religious beliefs and practices such as Jihad in Islam and creating a Buddhist states in Thailand, Sri Lanka and Burma (Myanmar) that would as well include policies that would be coherent with the force being applied to do the work. This goal might appear difficult to achieve; however, it is a realistic and achievable goal that would attain a durable or lasting result. There is a common saying that "if you think education is costly; try ignorance." Remember, ignorance is more expensive than education, it might even cost life.

4. Stop fighting terrorists with forces from outside terrorist countries. Fighting terrorism with military force is like killing someone who has being praying for death. Jihad in the Holy Qu'ran maintains that death is a treasure and precious than life. Osama bin Laden claims that Islamic nations are nations of "Martyrdom, the nations that desire death more than you desire life" (William, 2004:18). What could be the better theoretical explanation that made individuals to desire death more than life? The answer is simple. The extremists have been socialized and indoctrinated with Jihadic beliefs that their life after death will be more precious and bountiful with endless heavenly glorious wealth would be rewarded to them by Allah: with this Islamic Jihad, extremists perception of life and their action towards their utopist expected glory, we might want to relate to Julian Rotter (1954) behavioral theory that suggests that the expected result of a behavior has impact of the urge of individual to engage in the

behavior. In this case, the extremists or terrorist believe that the result of their behaviors will be heavenly glory and Allah being pleased with then give them the urge to engage in terrorist activities. Social Learning theories of Rotter, Gabriel Trade (1843–1904) and Albert Bandura can better help us gain insight into Islamic extremists' behaviors and institutionalize the appropriate behavioral modification techniques that would ameliorate the current and future global crisis. Democratic torchbearers should institutionalize using allies from terrorist infested area like Pakistan, Afghanistan, Iraq, and countries with terrorist cells organizations to get rid or minimize terrorism. Carefully invest in the allies to combat terrorist; monitor and evaluate their progress in the campaign and be willing to make midway changes if necessary. In order to understand this recommendation, you may want to outlook this illustration: The problem with terrorism is like a doctor trying to cure a sickness; doctors treat every sickness from within with any form of medication; be it injection or capsule. Even skin cancers or other skin diseases are treated from within the body, not outside. Why do you think doctors treat illnesses from within the body? This is food for thought.

As we have been informed theoretically that individuals affect their environments as well as their environments affect them, the culture of war or any from of violence can create negative irresistible impacts on human's behavior. According to the psychological and socio-cultural perspectives of understanding human behaviors, "past and present live encounters such as illness, natural disasters, war, physical and sexual abuses, domestic violence, divorce, poverty, the death of love ones, parental influences, frustration etc." are some negative consequences of the environment that determine human's behavior (Kassin, 1998: 608). When violence prolongs in a given society for a period of time, it evolves and be perceives as normal, and thereby becomes a culture or a way of life of that society. Jihad is a culture of Islam that is being passed from one generation to another, and this culture has been inhibited as a result of frustration that history accounts it as far as 610 AD when the Prophet Muhammad gave birth to the Islamic religion and the new religion came under strong criticism by the Quraysh in Mecca. The Prophet used militancy to conquer those anti Islam. Since the Prophet's victory over anti Islam in the Arabia region, the violence means in which he won was accepted as normal and a way of life of Islam believers. Prophet Muhammad engaged in battle with his hometown people out of frustration; hence, Muslim extremists and other groups who engage in terrorism maintained that their behavior is a result of frustration. For example, Osama claims that Islam extremists resulted to terrorism because the United States attacked the Muslims in Palestine, Somalia, as well as exploits their natural resources; America military occupation in Arab nations in the Arabian Peninsula; the twenty five years civil crisis between the Sinhalese Buddhist dominated government and the Tamils LTTE in Sri Lanka; the violence between military elitist and the anti government group in Burma (Myanmar) are all result of frustration, poverty, death or killing of love ones that are inextinguishable psychological and socio-cultural determinant of human's behavior.

As you can see, through our intellectual microscopic analysis of the emerging global terrorism, we are able to diagnose that religious beliefs and cultural practices that are crucial in human socialization in the environment steamed up as causes of global terror. Therefore, democracy torchbearers working with ally nations to formulate non violence policies; providing opportunities abroad to youths in Muslim dominated countries to learn modern democratic civilization and return to their individual countries would be positive reinforcement that would help modify the present unacceptable terrorist behaviors thereby produce a manageable social order.

BIBLIOGRAPHY

1. Jacob Neusner (1986). The Oral Torah: The Sacred Books of Judaism. Harper & Row, Publishers, San Francisco
2. Kenneth Atkinson (2004). Religions of the World: Judaism. Chelsea House Publishers
3. Angela Wood (1987). Judaism, B.T. Batsford Limited, London
4. Is Islam a Religion of War or Peace? (2001), Greenhaven Press
5. Walid Phares (2007) Jihadism Against Democracy: The Wars of Ideas; Palgrave MacMillan, New York, and Houndmills, Basingstoke, Hampshire, England
6. Maulana Muhammad Lli (1994). The Holy Qur'an, Ahmadiyyah Anjuman Isha'at Islam, Lahore, U.S.A.
7. Stephen Schwartz (2002). The Two Faces of Islam, Random House, New York
8. Paul Fregosi (1998). Jihad in the West, Prometheus Books, Amherst, N.Y.
9. Andrew G. Bostom, MD (2005). The Legacy of Jihad: Islam Holy War and the Fate of Non-Muslims; Prometheus Books, Amherst, NY
10. Carl Zimmer (2005). Smithsonian Intimate Guide to Human Origins, Harper Collins Publishers, New York
11. George Sullivan (1980). Discovery Archaeology: an Introduction to the Tools and Techniques of Archaeological Fieldwork, Doubleday & Company, Inc. Garden City, NY
12. Peter N. Peregrine (2003). World Prehistory: Two Million Years of Human life, Pearson Education, Inc. Upper Saddle River, NJ
13. H. Byron Earhart (1993). Religious Traditions of the World. Harper Collins Publishers, New York
14. Henry R. Luce et al. (1968). The World's Great Religions. Golden Press Inc., New York
15. Jeff Hay (2006). Religions and Religious Movements: Hinduism. Greenheaven Press, Farmington Hills, MI
16. Klostermaier K. Klaus (1998). Hinduism: A Short Introduction. Oneworld Publications, Oxford, England
17. Julian Rotter (1954). Social Learning and Clinical Psychology. Prentice Hall.

18. Albert Bandura (1977). Social Learning Theory. General Learning Press.

19. Ron Geaves (2006). Key Words in Hinduism. Georgetown University Press, Washington, DC

20. Gavin Flood (1996). An Introduction to Hinduism. Press Syndicate of the University of Cambridge, New York

21. Judith E. Walsh (2006). A Brief History of India. InfoBase Publishing, New York

22. Ramachandra Guha (2007). India After Gandhi: the History of World's Largest Democracy. HarperCollins Publisher, New York.

23. Carol S. Dweck (2006). Mind Set: The New Psychology of Success. Random House Inc.

24. Larry J. Siegel (2002). Criminology: The Core. Wadsworth/Thomson Learning, Belmont, CA

25. Clarke B. Peter, PhD (1993). The World's Religions: Understanding the Living Faiths. The Reader's Digest Association, Inc. Pleasantville, NY/ Montreal

26. Joe M. Schriver (2004). Human Behavior and the Social Environment. Pearson Education, Inc., Boston

27. Mary P. Fisher (2002). Living Religions. Prentice-Hall Inc. Upper Saddle River, NJ

28. Edward Rice (1973). The Five Great Religions. Four Winds Press, a division of Scholastic Magazines, Inc., New York

29. Richard Cavendish (1980). The Great Religions. Arco Publishing, Inc., New York

30. Ron Geaves (2006). Key Words in Christianity. Georgetown University Press, Washington D C

31. James M. Kouzes & Barry Z. Posner (2002). The Leadership Challenge. A Willey Imprint, San Francisco

32. Paul Tillich (1968). A History of Christian Thought. Harper & Row, Publishers, Inc., New York

33. Paul Johnson (1976). A History of Christianity. Simon & Schuster, New York.

34. Michael Martin (1991). The Case Against Christianity. Temple University Press, Philadelphia

35. James Morrison, M.D. (1995). DSM-IV Made Easy: The Clinician's Guide to Diagnosis. The Guilford Press, New York

36. Wayne A. Meeks (1986). The Moral World of the First Christians. The Westminster Press, Philadelphia

37. Owen Chadwick (1995). A History of Christianity. St. Martin's Press, New York

38. Alfreda P. Iglehart and Rosina M. Becerra (2000). Social Service and the Ethnic Community. Waveland Press, Inc.,Long Grove, IL

39. Joseph E. B. Lumbard 2004). Islam, Fundamentalism, and the Betrayal of Tradition. World Wisdom, Inc., Bloomington, IN

40. Sachiko Murata and William C. Chittick (1994). The Vision of Islam. Paragon House, New York

41. Joseph S. Nye, Jr. (2002). Understanding International Conflicts: An Introduction to Theory and History. The Maple-Vail Book Manufacturing Group

42. Rohan Gunaratna (2002). Inside Al Qaeda: Global Network of Terror. The Berkley Publishing Group, New York

43. Seyyed Hossein Nasr (2002). The Heart of Islam: Enduring Values for Humanity. HarperCollins Publishers, New York.

44. Noble Ross Reat (1994). Religion of the World. Buddhism, A History. Asian Humanities Press, Berkeley, CA

45. Veronica Ions (1986). Library of the World's Myths and Legends. Indian Mythology. Hamlyn Publishing Group Limited.

46. Donald S. Lopez, Jr. (2001). HarperCollins Publishers, New York

47. John F.Longres (1990). Human Behavior in the Social Environment. F. E. Peacock Publishers, Itasca, IL.

48. Geoffrey Parrinder (1984). The World Religions from Ancient History to Present. Facts on File, New York

49. Patrick Peebles (2006). The History of Sri Lanka. Greenwood Press, Westport, CT

50. Dalai Lama (1999). Ethics for the New Millennium. Penguin Putnam Inc., New York

51. Andrew Powell (1989). Harmony Books, New York.

52. Nira Wickramasinghe (2006). Sri Lanka in the Modern Age: A History of Contested Identities. University of Hawaii Press, Honolulu

53. Heinrich Dumoulin and John C. Maraldo (1976). The Cultural, Political, and Religious Significance of Buddhism in the Modern World. Macmillan Publishing Co., New York

54. Bernard-Henri Levy (2004). War, Evil, and the End of History. Melville House Publishing, Hoboken, NJ.

55. Joseph S. Nye Jr. (2003). Understanding International Conflict: an Introduction to Theory and History, Fourth Edition. Harvard University

56. Heinrich Dumoulin and John C. Maraldo (1976). The Cultural, Political, and Religious Significance of Buddhism in the Modern World. Macmillan Publishing Co., Inc., New York

57. Thant Myint-U (2006). The River of Lost Footsteps: Histories of Burma. Farrar, Straus and Giroux, New York

58. Frederick M. Bunge (1983). Burma, a Country Study. Headquarters, Department of the Army, DA Pam 550-61

59. James Mawdsley (2001). The Iron Road: A Stand for Truth and Democracy in Burma. North Point Press, New York

60. The Dalai Lama (2001). An Open Heart. Little, Brown and Company, Boston. New York. London

61. Aung San Suu Kyi (1991). Freedom from Fear and other Writings. Penguin Group, New York

62. Paul L. Williams (2004). Osama's Revenge: The Next 9/11, What the Media and the Government Haven't Told You. Prometheus Books, Amherst, NY

63. Saul Kassin (1998). Psychology, Second Edition. Prentice-Hall, Inc. Simon & Schuster/ A Viacom Company, Upper Saddle River, NJ

INDEX·

A

Absolutist 47, 49, 54, 70, 86
Academic disciplines ix
African, Africa 21, 47, 70, 71, 72, 73, 74, 75, 76, 77, 79, 80, 95
Alexandria 72
Allah 13, 14, 21, 23, 25, 26, 27, 28, 29, 30, 31, 35, 44, 109, 110, 113, 114
Al Qaeda 23
An eye for an eye 6, 34
Anglo-Burmese war 96, 102
Arabia 18, 20, 23, 24, 69, 109, 115
Arabian Peninsula 15, 21, 49, 115
Archibald Colquhoun 95
Aristocracy 102
Aryans invasion 52
Authoritarianism began to 76

B

Battlefront for God 9
Belief ix, xi, xiii, xv, xvi, xvii, 1, 2, 3, 4, 6, 8, 9, 10, 15, 16, 18, 19, 20, 21, 23, 25, 32, 36, 38, 39, 46, 48, 51, 52, 53, 54, 57, 59, 63, 66, 69, 70, 71, 72, 73, 74, 75, 76, 77, 78, 82, 84, 90, 92, 97, 98, 101, 103, 104, 108, 113, 115
British 45, 48, 49, 55, 88, 95, 96, 97, 101
British domination 55, 97, 101
Buddhism iii, v, ix, xi, 9, 21, 46, 52, 81, 82, 83, 84, 85, 86, 87, 88, 89, 90, 91, 93, 94, 95, 97, 98, 99, 100, 101, 103, 104, 105
Buddhism has three major sects 97
Burma 69, 85, 86, 90, 94, 95, 96, 97, 98, 99, 100, 101, 102, 103, 104, 113

C

Celestial divinity 58
Charles Darwin's theory of evolution 39

Charles Taylor 47
China 69, 94, 95, 104
Christ 38, 57, 58, 59, 61, 63, 66, 69, 78, 79, 109
Christianity iii, v, ix, xi, xvi, 8, 9, 11, 15, 16, 21, 38, 44, 46, 47, 52, 55, 57, 58, 59, 61, 63, 65, 68, 69, 70, 72, 73, 74, 75, 76, 77, 78, 84, 89, 93, 101, 105, 109
CMC 91
Colombo privileged minority 88
Coming together of Jews 2
Conduit through 11, 72, 105
Constitution 10, 86, 89, 91, 93, 94, 103, 112, 113
Consultative ideology 17
Contemporary 1, 2, 7, 13, 16, 17, 24, 31, 35, 36, 38, 39, 41, 45, 50, 51, 52, 112
Contextual understanding of xiii, xiv
Culture ix, xiii, xiv, xv, xvi, 1, 3, 4, 6, 8, 9, 10, 17, 18, 19, 20, 21, 23, 25, 34, 38, 39, 40, 43, 46, 51, 52, 53, 54, 55, 57, 62, 63, 64, 65, 69, 70, 73, 74, 75, 76, 77, 80, 85, 86, 87, 96, 97, 101, 102, 104, 105, 108, 110, 112, 114
Customs xiii, xv, 1, 2, 3, 4, 8, 17, 18, 19, 57

D

Dalai Lama 90, 100
David Dakake 30
Democracy ix, xiii, xiv, xv, xvi, xvii, 1, 2, 4, 6, 7, 8, 10, 11, 13, 15, 16, 17, 18, 20, 22, 23, 25, 33, 35, 36, 38, 40, 41, 42, 43, 44, 45, 46, 47, 48, 52, 55, 58, 63, 68, 69, 72, 73, 74, 77, 78, 79, 81, 83, 85, 86, 88, 101, 102, 108, 111, 112, 115
Democracy as a System xvi

www.ingramcontent.com/pod-product-compliance
Lightning Source LLC
Chambersburg PA
CBHW020239290526
45784CB00003B/1037